The Way We Let Them Go

A Corporate Cheerleader's Guide to Layoffs

Corporate Cheerleader Guides

Sara Bovey Covey

THE CORPORATE
CHEERLEADER

For the ones who cheered when I couldn't.

Through every layoff, every restart, every rise —

You rekindled my spirit, so I could share it to lift others.

Contents

The Way We Let Them Go

Supplemental Materials

Workbook Companion

The Way We Let Them Go

Preface

I never wanted to write this book. I wanted to write about leadership in the joyful moments. Things like...

- When your team crushes a goal you've worked toward for months
- When someone finally steps into the promotion they've earned ten times over
- When a once-quiet employee speaks up and commands a room as the leader you always thought he or she could be

These are the moments that fill your cup, the ones that keep you invested in the work when the meetings are long, the metrics are murky, and the politics feel heavier than the progress. They're the memories you carry into performance reviews, mentoring calls, and interviews when someone asks, "What kind of leader are you?"

They're the moments I thought I'd write about. Here's the truth, though: lead people long enough, and you'll eventually walk into that *other* kind of moment.

The kind with silence.

The kind with resignation or disbelief in someone's eyes.

The kind where you're not leading someone toward something but *out of* something.

Perhaps you're holding a clipboard, reading from a script approved by Legal and HR as the person left in the room when the role ends, but the ripple effect of what had happened doesn't. In moments like these, everything you thought you knew about leadership changes.

What about all the books and trainings, and leadership podcasts? Unfortunately, they don't really cover this part.

Will they tell you how to develop high-potential talent, inspire innovation, and have difficult conversations when someone's underperforming? Sure! What they *won't* tell you, though, is what to do when someone isn't underperforming at all and still being let go. They won't tell you how to maintain eye contact while delivering news set to change someone's financial reality, identity, and trust in the company—possibly forever. They won't teach you how to close the laptop, steady your hands, and walk back into a team meeting after you just abruptly snatched someone's job away in the blink of an eye.

There's no guidebook for how to keep your values intact while carrying out a decision you didn't make in the first place—or maybe one you did but still lost sleep over. There's no business school lecture on how to manage your face while someone is crying, too stunned to speak, or simply looks at you and says, "I thought we were doing well." No onboarding packet, likewise, will prepare you to deliver a message that ends with someone packing up his or her work life into a cardboard box.

That's precisely why this book exists.

Because the clipboard moment? It's real, it's common, and it's mostly unsupported. Please know this, though: you are not a bad leader if you find yourself in that same moment. In fact, your leadership is more important there than anywhere else.

I didn't stumble into this work. My perspective comes from living every side of the layoff table.

I started in HR through a niche agency recruiting. As the agency grew, they tapped me to build a training program and lead corporate recruiting. I was thriving—until a merger made my role redundant, and I found myself laid off for the first time.

From there, I moved into dental as a Talent Acquisition Manager and Immigration Liaison. That's where I met the mentor who would change my career—she brought me into manufacturing, where I redefined recruitment, built training programs, and served as the HR Business Partner for a local facility. Then COVID hit. The business shifted, the facility closed, and once again, I was in the thick of layoffs—supporting managers through individual conversations, sometimes sitting across the table alone. Eventually, I was laid off myself.

I landed next in logistics as an HR Business Partner. Within a year, a needs analysis presentation led me to a Senior Program Manager role in Talent Management. For three years, I partnered with leaders navigating layoffs— listening to what worked, what didn't, and what they wished they could do differently.

I remember the first time I sat in the room as HR support, just there to "handle the process." In real terms, that meant printing separation paperwork and standing by silently while someone's professional world exploded in front of them.

I can still feel it: my heart pounding, not out of fear of conflict, but from knowing exactly what was about to happen—and having no tools to soften the blow. The meeting lasted maybe three minutes. No questions, just a nod and a shaky "Okay."

When he turned to me for answers I didn't have the power to give, it cut deeper than when it had happened to me personally. Because this time, I knew it could have been done better.

That's when I made myself a promise:

If I'm going to be in the room, I'm going to be fully human in that room.

Later, when I was the one holding the clipboard, leading— not just supporting—the conversation, I carried every emotion with me: disappointment, confusion, anger, sometimes even relief. I wrote the scripts, practiced the timing, and steadied my own voice. Then I had to walk back into the workplace, leading a team left shaken but still standing.

What I needed most in those moments wasn't another policy checklist. I had those.

What I needed was perspective. Someone to remind me:

- You can do this with dignity.
- You can honor your values while honoring your responsibilities.
- You can be clear and still care.

- You can lead through this without turning cold or falling apart.

That's when I began writing the guide I wished I had—the one I now offer to you.

This book is not a tactical checklist (though you'll find practical tools in it) nor an HR compliance manual (though I respect those who write them). It's a leadership companion for the most difficult conversations you'll ever have with your team.

Dig into it before the meeting, skim it the night before the big news drops, or go back and do some underlining after a long day of awkward 1:1s. Make it the one you return to when you wonder if you handled something right—or what you should do the next time.

I wrote this book for...

- The leader who still believes people matter, even when business pressures make it hard to remember
- The leader who cries in the car but shows up to the meeting nice and composed

- The leader who knows layoffs are sometimes necessary, but they're *never just a transaction*
- YOU!

Since you're reading this right now, chances are you've already walked someone out or are about to. Maybe you're managing the fog that settles over a team after someone disappears from the org chart and/or feeling:

- Guilty for doing your job
- Angry due to how the message was handed to you
- Grief-stricken by your inability to protect everyone
- Numbness from the need to "be fine" in front of your team.

You are not broken or failing; you're just a human doing hard things—quietly, behind the scenes, and with more integrity than anyone may ever know.

This book exists to help you do these hard things *well* via language, clarity, empathy, and a plan. Because here's the part no one talks about: when the dust from the layoff settles, what remains is your leadership legacy—not the announcement nor the spreadsheets but instead how you made people feel when they were at their most vulnerable: how you showed up when someone's world shifted, helped your team move forward without erasing those who left, carried the culture when the structure changed, and held your own heart in the middle of it.

If you're holding the clipboard—literally or figuratively—or have ever said "I want to do this better," this book is for you.

So, let's talk about what "better" can look like as we walk you through the planning, the message, the moment, and the aftermath: preparing you not just for the layoff itself but for the emotional weight it will no doubt carry long after the meeting wraps up, making space for real leadership. Leadership that's quiet, steady, honest, and grounded, and isn't afraid to say:

"This is hard. I don't have all the answers, but I will show up."

With heart (and pom-poms),

Sara Bovey Covey

Your Corporate Cheerleader

Introduction

Leadership isn't something you switch on during a layoff.
It's something you practice every day—and it shows up loudest when things get hard.

This book isn't about what to do *after* a layoff but instead what it means to lead *through* one—and like it matters. Layoffs, after all, don't begin when someone is let go. The moment someone whispers, "We may need to make cuts" and the idea plants itself in budget meetings and spreadsheet columns, it's there. Layoffs gain shape in calendar invites, missing context, and hallway tension and are remembered not just for who was impacted but for how *you* showed up amidst it all.

Leadership is Constant. Layoffs Simply Reveal the Same.

If you're holding this book, you already know: a layoff is not just a business moment. It's a leadership moment. A legacy moment, if you will: one you're a part of even if you weren't the one who made the decision impacting the people who will tote it along in their minds for the rest of their careers.

You're the one delivering, explaining, and/or rebuilding after the news. More than that, your team is watching as the broader culture shifts. Your presence—or, otherwise, absence—will echo through the halls you all walk.

You don't lead a layoff like a one-time event. You lead it like how you lead everything else, via habits, preparation, presence, and care. That's what this book is about: not how to steer clear of the difficult decisions but instead how to navigate them with a sense of humanity, showing up when your team needs you rather than spinning a layoff in your or your company's favor. Not about softening the blow, it's about leading with integrity even when people are hurting.

Holding Contradictions

Layoffs, like leadership, are rarely clean. You will be asked to:

- Be strong, yet soft
- Deliver the facts, yet hold all the feelings
- Center people, yet still serve the business
- Take accountability for a decision you may not have made yourself
- Support those who are leaving while rebuilding trust with those who stay

Let's sit with these tensions—on purpose! Real leadership lives in the in-between.

You might feel whiplash. One chapter might empower you to speak up. The next? Tell you to stay quiet and listen. That's not confusion but context and the same kind of leadership most people are never taught.

How Is the Book Structured?

Eleven core chapters cover the layoff lifecycle from every leadership angle, teaching you how to...

- Prepare your team before a change is even on the table
- Build roles that are exit-ready without guilt
- Deliver hard news without robotic detachment
- Communicate with clarity and compassion
- Re-engage a team that feels rattled or left behind
- Recover your own energy and realign your priorities

- Leave people feeling whole—even when you couldn't keep them

You'll also find:

- A workbook with activities, tools, and guided reflections
- Special appendices featuring emotional response tools, tips for addressing layoff complaints, HR insights, and a leadership self-check
- And, at the end, your framework for leading every hard moment the best way possible

Is There a Model?

Yes, there's a model, and a darn good one at that. **CHEER**, a repeatable, flexible leadership framework, is shorthand for what it means to lead with clarity, care, and courage during the hardest moments—but you won't find it in Chapter 1.

Why?

Because this book isn't about memorizing acronyms. It's about building muscle. You'll learn the model by walking through what it means, practicing the presence, and showing up in the mess. When we get there and the model appears, it'll feel like naming something you already knew but never had the words to express. That's how we'll tie the bow, not with spin but with structure, affirming your leadership legacy.

Who This Book Is For

Are you a/an...

- Leader who's had to walk someone out, maybe for the first time?
- Manager who stayed behind and held the clipboard, wondering how to hold your team together?
- HR Business Partner who wrote the talking points and stayed silent while someone else read them?
- Executive who approved the strategy but still felt your stomach drop when the names were finalized?
- Person who's personally experienced a layoff and wants to make sure you do better?

This book is for *you*!

How to Use This Book

Read it front to back, back to front, or jump to the chapter you need right here and right now. Underline it. Dog-ear it. Bring it to your next 1:1. Use the workbook. Share the reflection prompts. Teach your team to lead better, too.

Introduction

And when things feel heavy? Return to the parts that remind you you don't have to be perfect; you just have to be *present*. Clear. Courageous. Compassionate. A cheerleader, not for the moment but for the person inside it.

Let's begin, jumping into not only the book but a new way of leading—especially when it matters most.

1

The Truth About Layoffs Nobody Tells You

It always starts the same way.

A message that looks harmless. A phrase that lands like a stone.

"Do you have time to talk?"

Even now, those five words still tighten my chest. They've prefaced three of the most defining—and devastating—moments of my career.

The first time, the call ended as abruptly as it began. I was released on the spot. No conversation, no transition plan—just an efficient ending to years of commitment. I used my personal email to close out my workload because I couldn't bear to leave things unfinished. It was fast, final, and dehumanizing.

The second time, the facility I worked for was shutting down. But this time, my manager handled it differently— with grace. She gave me time and space to transition my work, a firm end date, and a stay bonus. It was still hard, but it was human. It reminded me that endings could be done with dignity.

The third time, it wasn't a conversation — it was choreography. A script delivered with composure so controlled it felt like strategy, not sincerity. I was told there would be time, though the definition of that shifted as things unfolded. It's a strange kind of grief — being erased in real time while still expected to perform. When the end finally came, it was quiet, procedural, and somehow still anticlimactic.

By then, I knew the rhythm of it all too well—the careful phrasing, the clipped tone, the sudden finality that turns years of purpose into minutes of paperwork.

Three different moments. Three different leaders.

Each started with the same question—and each one changed me.

Because when you've given your whole heart to an organization, and it's handed back to you without ceremony, something in you rewires. You start to wonder if care and clarity can coexist. You start to question if endings can ever be done well.

I should have known better, in theory. I'd been in the room before—the other side of the conversation. I'd helped plan layoffs, coach managers, and write the talking points meant to make hard messages land softer. I'd supported the logistics, the legalities, and the leadership. I'd stood behind the scenes when the comms plan went live and the spreadsheets were finalized.

I've also been the one walking through rows of desks with manila envelopes in hand, holding my breath for the reactions I couldn't control. I've been the calm one, the clear one, the composed one.

Nothing—absolutely nothing—could've prepared me for what it feels like to be the one whose role is slashed, though. No amount of policy experience or HR process knowledge preps you for the moment when your name becomes a line item. It doesn't prepare you for...

- The hollow feeling that creeps into your chest
- How everything feels quiet and loud at the same time
- The way your body feels heavy and your inbox feels irrelevant

And it especially doesn't prepare you for how quickly your role disappears from the conversation, as if it were never yours at all.

That's the moment when the professional becomes personal—when the system you've served feels suddenly foreign. You realize that for all the care you've tried to design into processes, leadership itself can still fail the moment it matters most.

When Leadership Fails the Moment

To be clear, it was never just about the layoffs themselves. It was about how they were done—or, more accurately, how they weren't.

Each one revealed something different about leadership.

- One was swift with some acknowledgment, handled like a task to be checked off.
- One was handled with care, proof that even hard moments can be done well.
- And one was all script, no substance— delivered as if empathy were optional.

Layoffs, after all, can and will happen. They're a reality of work and not always avoidable. Sometimes they make sense and are necessary for a business to stay afloat, pivot, or survive.

The delivery, though, is a choice. It's where leadership either rises to meet the weight of the moment—or collapses under it.

And when leaders fail that moment, they don't just miss an opportunity to be kind. They send a message about what— and who—truly matters. Sometimes that message is quiet but unmistakable: *You are replaceable.* Other times, it's even louder: *You don't matter here.*

That's the wound most people carry—not the layoff itself, but the way they were made to feel in the process.

The Impact Beyond the Exit

Here's the truth: layoffs hit everyone. Even if your name isn't on the list, the culture around you shifts nonetheless as people are left to wonder...

- "Will I be next?"
- "Does my work matter?"
- "Can I trust leadership anymore?"

Layoffs, when done poorly, don't just affect the spreadsheet. They affect the very soul of an organization and shake trust, sever loyalty, and leave behind emotional residue.

Even when a layoff makes perfect business sense, how it's handled still defines the moment. Because people don't remember the spreadsheet—they remember the silence, the tone, and how quickly the warmth left the room. I've watched great leaders steady a team with honesty and presence, and I've seen others shrink behind policy and speed. One choice rebuilds trust; the other breaks it for good.

That's the real work of leadership: showing people that

even when the outcome can't change, how they're treated still can.

The Cost of Silence, Speed, and Spin

Layoffs, much too often, are rushed: announced in broad strokes with little context, sanitized language, and a promise to "support everyone through the transition." What does that actually mean, though?

We've been trained to avoid the uncomfortable moments, to keep it short and clinical, and get it over with quickly while letting HR do the rest. Here's what I've learned, though: short and vague isn't kind but *incomplete*. When the layoff moments happen and incomplete leadership inevitably fails, it creates cultural scars that never fade.

What people remember extends beyond being let go to *how* they were let go...

- Was the conversation rushed?
- Did their manager seem to care?
- Was there dignity in the goodbye?
- Were their contributions acknowledged?

This book, likewise, isn't a bitter book but a *better* book. Better conversations. Better planning. Better leadership in the moments where it matters most. Because when everything feels unstable and you're the one who's supposed to steady the team, you need more than a talking point. You need a framework, a voice, and a plan keeping people at the center.

At the end of the day, layoffs aren't just moments of transition but moments of truth. How we navigate them determines who we are as leaders—not just who we *say* we are. This means...

- Leading with clarity *and* compassion
- Delivering hard messages without losing your humanity
- Holding structure without crushing the person on the other end of the call

This, my friends, is indeed possible!

Remember...

The spreadsheet doesn't feel. The people do.

2

How We Got Here (a Business Case for Broken Hearts)

Hurt.

That's where it started—not with anger nor denial but with that slow, sharp ache that comes when something lands exactly the way you expected it to but still knocks the wind out of you.

Interestingly, there were other times before each layoff, when it might've made more strategic sense to let me go—maybe when the program I was running shifted into maintenance mode or a high-demand project cycle ended and the pace slowed to something more manageable, for example. I've worked in enough operational settings, after all, to know how such decisions play out. When the need lessens, so too does the justification for some roles. It's just the business of bandwidth.

I would've understood back then and maybe even agreed,

but when they finally made the decision—when I was midprogram, launching a new project, at the culmination of months of work—it didn't feel like business but instead like a dismissal, a convenient reorg masked as strategic vision.

I wasn't just running projects but was in fact midstream during an enterprise-wide rollout with my fingerprints on every slide, every conversation, every strategic angle. I was in the middle of it all, and yet, there I was: being asked to pass the baton with no track, no warm-up, and (on two occasions) no teammate's hand to grab it.

The people they assigned my work to were already stretched too thin. Don't get me wrong: they were smart, capable, and dedicated employees. They just didn't have the bandwidth. In assigning my legacy to overworked colleagues without the time or context necessary to sustain it, they didn't just move the role—they set the work up to fail. Not a strategy, it was detachment disguised as decisiveness and made me feel disposable in the process.

Strategy Confused with Detachment

In many organizations—especially those under pressure to scale or appease external expectations—layoffs have become a kind of symbolic move. Make a bold cut. Streamline the structure. Signal alignment with market forces. Show decisiveness. Internally, it's often discussed in metaphors...

- "Move the chess pieces."
- "Realign the fleet."
- "Right-size the org."
- "Clean the slate."

These phrases aren't evil in their own right but become a form of "emotional bypassing" when they're used without care: arming leaders with the ability to feel some semblance of control while removing any sort of human cost from the language. To be clear, the failure doesn't lie in the decision to restructure. Sometimes roles do outgrow the needs of the business, just as there are real budget realities and/or the lack of a need for a specific position. When these decisions are made—or delivered—with no thought for the person whose whole life is upended in the process, however, this is where the failure exists.

We've let detachment become synonymous with professionalism and convinced ourselves that being unaffected is a leadership trait, but what if it's not? What if being affected is a sign that you're still human in the process? What if being present and steady is a better indicator of strength than being numb? What if care and clarity belong in the same sentence?

What if...

How Care Got Cut from the Process

Corporate culture has streamlined the layoff playbook over the years, something that involves...

- Timing the announcement
- Preparing the script
- Coordinating with legal
- Drafting internal comms
- Establishing exit logistics
- Controlling the narrative

It's a well-oiled machine—efficient, predictable, and executable—yet we've likewise managed to squeeze out the most important piece in this pursuit of precision: *care*.

Layoffs are now events to manage rather than moments to lead, measured by an absence of leaks or how quickly the transition is executed. No one seems to measure, though, how deeply trust is broken, how long the culture will suffer, or how many high performers start quietly updating their résumés in the aftermath.

In trying to make layoffs clean, we've made them cold: removing the space for emotion in the name of "keeping things professional." The truth is, though, that layoffs aren't operations but experiences. They're lived, felt, and remembered. In stripping them of care, we replace humanity with harm.

The Script Ends - the Impact Doesn't

For the person being laid off, there's no...

- Space to process
- Time to ask thoughtful questions
- Acknowledgment of what they contributed
- Pathway to understand how they went from being a "critical contributor" to a calendar invite

There's the meeting on the calendar, the link, the message. And then? Silence.

The manager delivering the message, meanwhile, rarely has support for the emotional fallout or any real coaching on how to navigate what happens *after* the script wraps up. What he/she *does* have, however, is a thank-you and a calendar shift. The team left behind often has no context (just absence, speculation, and the reallocation of work to already-filled plates), with HR there to absorb the fallout, manage the logistics, and hold the silence as the face of the layoff, even when leadership made the decision. We become the cleanup crew and are by no means equipped to do it alone.

The Myth of the "Clean Cut"

Layoffs are rarely one-time events that occur in some sort of emotional silo. After all, you don't deliver the news and move on, nor can you wipe the impact clean with a severance package and a talking point. You think you're making one decision, but it ripples and affects...

- Trust
- Engagement
- Retention
- What your team believes you'll do next time

Morale doesn't return with a pizza party or a town hall, with trust unable to rebuild on its own. If you don't name what just happened, people will write their own story and fill in the blanks with fear, frustration, or both. That's not resistance; it's *human* and not a return to "normal" but the beginning of a new emotional baseline. Leadership in this same space defines what happens next.

HR Can't Be the Sole Culture Keeper

Culture is too often assigned to HR, who in turn simply can't repair what leadership neglects. Can we coach, script, support, and absorb? Sure thing! What we *can't* do, however, is carry the credibility of others. When layoffs happen, people don't look to HR for reassurance; they look to their leaders, direct managers, and the people they see on their calendar every week. Culture is built through daily interactions and tested in critical ones, with people not remembering the HR email but instead how you looked when you delivered the news. They'll remember if you said their name with care and if you stayed present or rushed the message.

HR can guide the process, but you, as the messenger, own the moment.

Layoffs Are Leadership Moments

There's something you need to hear clearly: You don't get to separate yourself from the experience just because someone else made the final call. Even if you weren't in the strategy meetings, didn't build the spreadsheet, and/or "just found out yesterday," your team sees you as part of it —and you are!

That doesn't mean you're to blame, but just that you're responsible for how you show up now. People won't remember your level or proximity to the decision. What they will remember is your *presence*. Did you look them in the eye? Did you offer clarity (or deflect) and hold space for emotion? Did you care?

It's a defining moment, not just for them but for *you*.

What I'm NOT Saying

Let's not confuse things! What I'm sharing here isn't about...

- A call to keep everyone

- Shielding underperformers or resisting necessary change
- Pretending layoffs won't hurt, no matter how carefully you handle them

Instead, it's simply about doing the difficult thing well—with clarity, compassion, and intention —restoring dignity to a process reduced to damage control, while recognizing that every layoff is more than a line item, as it's a *life* you're touching. This deserves so much more than a script.

There's a Better Way

We can't always control the outcome, but we *can* control the experience. When layoffs are handled with care...

- People may still grieve—but they won't feel discarded.
- People may still hurt—but they won't question their worth.
- People may still leave—but they won't have a lasting wound.

That's the bar: not perfection but presence.

We don't need to turn layoffs into therapy sessions or steer clear of the hard decisions, but we *do* need to stop acting like empathy is incompatible with execution.

Empathy is the skill. Clarity is the leadership. Care is the differentiator. As for courage? That's choosing to lead in the moment, *especially* when it would simply be easier to hide behind the process. This chapter, thus, is the wake-up call that invites you to slow down and ask: *What kind of leader do I want to be when the call comes?*

Don't worry! There are plenty of tools, words, and frameworks to follow.

Remember...

How you lay someone off is how he or she will remember you. Lead accordingly.

3
Great Leaders Know Everyone Leaves

Most leadership advice about exits sounds like crisis management: layoffs, restructures, sudden resignations, etc. The truth is, though, that every person on your team will leave their role eventually—whether for growth or family or to go back to school, start their own thing, or simply to rest. People leave for promotions, babies, burnouts, retirement, relocation, heartbreak, or health; or maybe it's just time to try something new!

It's not failure but *movement*, and it's not your job to control it but to honor it, plan for it, and lead for it as if you always knew it was coming.

Not preparing for a reduction but simply for reality, you want to be the kind of leader who builds...

- Teams that feel safe to grow
- Systems that don't collapse with a two-week notice
- Cultures where people know they can leave well and be celebrated, not just replaced

This chapter gives you the blueprint to get there, not because people will leave but because they should be *allowed* to do so—and you should be ready when it happens!

Roles Designed to Be Left (and Lifted From)

If your team is one person away from disaster, you don't have a strategy; you have a dependency. One of the most practical ways to show care for your people is to plan for their exit before they ever consider leaving— not because you expect them to go but because you respect their journey if they decide to do so. This looks like...

- **Living Role Guides:** These quarterly updates document responsibilities, key systems, contacts, timelines, workflows, and "this only makes sense to me" quirks.
- **Successor Snapshots:** Identify who could step in with support. Who's shadowed the work? Who wants to grow into the role?
- **Relationship Maps:** Outline who the person partners with most, both internally and externally, and mention how strong the "handshakes" are.

Knowing where influence and collaboration live will make the transition smoother.

When you make it easy to pass the torch, you give people the freedom to step forward in the absence of any guilt AND protect your team from feeling blindsided.

Knowledge Sharing Normalized as Growth, Not Goodbye

Too many leaders treat documentation, cross-training, and delegation as red flags, as if prepping for someone else to do your job means you're already halfway out the door. Let's flip that narrative, knowing exit-readiness should be part of *every* employee's development plan regardless of tenure or intention, and build...

- **Process Libraries:** Not just SOPs, these practical tools (screenshots, timelines, metrics, pitfalls, and first steps) are there to help when things go wrong.
- **Naming Conventions + Shared Drives:** No more "final_final_reallyfinal_v4." Make files easy to find, interpret, and pick up.
- **Quarterly Cross-Training Rotations:** Give people short, structured time blocks to shadow roles outside their own. Not only does this build empathy and resilience, but it also sparks curiosity.
- **Legacy Logs:** Encourage team members to track useful contacts, project insights, wins, and lessons

learned for the person who'll occupy their seat someday.

It's not about the exit; it's about continuity. Prepping in this way helps people feel more valued when their work is designed to last and less panicked when life throws them a curveball.

Bandwidth Isn't Infinite; Lead with "Capacity Math"

Let's be clear: when someone leaves, *something* has to give. Their work doesn't just magically disappear or redistribute without consequence, nor can you pretend the system will operate at full strength after you remove a key player. Yet so many leaders do exactly that: reshuffling instead of reprioritizing, absorbing silently instead of acknowledging loss, and asking their team to "hang in there" instead of setting boundaries. Not leadership, it's slow-motion burnout ripe for actions the best leaders out there take, including...

- **Capacity Audits:** Check in often, knowing how many hours, how many projects, how much energy your people are expending—and what they're truly capable of sustaining.
- **"If/Then" Planning:** Create scenarios: *If* this person leaves, *then* these things are paused,

reassigned, or dropped. Build a list now, not in crisis.

- **Project Tiering:** Identify what's mission-critical, what's "important but can wait," and what's paused indefinitely. Revisit these often.
- **Prioritization Matrices:** Teach your team to make decisions based on impact and urgency—not noise, emotion, or seniority. Help them feel comfortable enough to say: "This is loud but not important."
- **Saying No Like a Grown-Up:** When a project doesn't fit your team's capacity, name it. Don't apologize for doing work sustainably. Leadership isn't martyrdom; it's stewardship.

Your job is to protect people and performance, which includes naming the limits—and sticking to them!

Managing the Message

We all say we want open, trusting cultures. Yet when someone hints at exploring other roles, we freeze up or worse—pull away. The bottom line is that you can't expect honesty if you punish transparency, which is why the best cultures out there make room for the *possibility* of departure—not because they want people to leave but because they want them to honestly express if they're considering it. You don't always have to know who's going next, but your team should know that if and when they *do* leave, they'll be met with grace, support, and celebration.

Try phrases like:

"If and when your path changes, I'll feel proud of what we've built together."

"We've designed this role to be passed on well, which means I'll support you when the time is right."

"Leaving doesn't mean you're letting us down, but instead that something is growing."

When someone gives notice:

- Celebrate them
- Ask for their assistance in evolving the role
- Let them help onboard the next person
- Show the team how departures are done with dignity

When people leave well, they don't just walk away; they walk *forward* and (bonus!) carry your leadership with them.

Permitting People to Evolve

Employees don't always leave because something went wrong. Sometimes, they leave because something went *right*. They grew, healed, and gained clarity about their wants and needs—your leadership giving them the space to figure it all out! Don't punish that. Celebrate it, knowing a great leader doesn't grip tightly and instead coaches forward while creating a culture that makes it normal for...

- Lateral moves to be applauded, not simply seen as sideways movement
- Growth to include exits, not just promotions
- Transition planning to be part of every performance cycle
- Sabbaticals, parental leave, mental health breaks, and graceful goodbyes to be seen as strength—not weakness

People aren't permanent, but they are precious. In feeling trusted to evolve, they'll dedicate their full selves to the role until it no longer fits—which is when they'll leave with stories of gratitude, not scars.

No Need to Hold Them Forever to Lead Them Well

Some of the best leaders I know have teams chock-full of alumni, former employees who still...

- Reach out for advice
- Refer great talent
- Sing their praises at conferences

Why? Because said leaders didn't try to trap their people. Instead, they *prepared* them, led with freedom, not fear, and created a culture where people could grow in *and* out of the role (and were loved through both).

Remember...

Your job is not to hold the seat—it's to light the path. Lead them well while you have them, and prepare them to soar when it's time.

4
Leading (Well!) When It All Gets Real

As I mentioned earlier, people leave companies for all kinds of reasons—some by choice, some by circumstance. *Your* job is to make sure they're supported either way.

Layoffs are one of the most emotionally charged forms of departure, but they're far from the only reason triggering an exit. People leave jobs because they've outgrown the role. Perhaps they're burned out, moving cross-country to care for a parent, adopting a new role as a stay-at-home parent, or finally found the courage to chase a dream. People leave for heartbreak. For healing. For joy. For newness. For rest.

You don't always get to choose why someone leaves, but you *do* get to choose how ready you are for that moment. Let's talk about the first five things great leaders do to prepare for this, not because they're paranoid but because they're purposeful.

They Build with the End in Mind

Rather than act as if people are permanent, great leaders build inherently transitional systems—designed to evolve, grow, and pass hands without falling apart. That means...

- Every role has documentation, not just "assumed" tasks
- Every process is shared knowledge, not gatekept experience
- Every person is supported in owning his or her work, not isolated in the same way

Building with the end in mind removes any drama from the exit. The team isn't shocked and projects don't collapse, giving the person leaving the wherewithal to pass the baton—not drop the ball!

The team doesn't fail when someone exits. You only fail if you've made that person impossible to replace.

They Normalize Cross-Training

Too many leaders treat cross-training as a reactive move, something we do when a person's already on the way out. It's too late then, however, meaning you should build cross-training into your team's *development strategy*—not as a warning but as a way to grow skills, confidence, and shared responsibility.

Set up quarterly "switch and learn" weeks. Build rotational knowledge exchange into regular workflows. Use job shadowing as a way to build depth *and* empathy. When everyone understands how adjacent roles work, you...

- Build trust across silos
- Reduce panic when someone's unavailable
- Prevent knowledge from living in just one person's brain
- Are you ready in case someone suddenly departs

Cross-training doesn't just protect your team from disruption; it builds loyalty! People stay where they feel confident, challenged, and capable.

They Audit & Document the Work

Process documentation gets a bad rap, often seen as tedious, overly formal, or something you'll "get to eventually." But in great teams? It's foundational. Create living documentation libraries that include...

- SOPs with clear steps, screenshots, and troubleshooting procedures
- Conventions are named to make things findable
- Clear folder structures that don't require a decoder ring

- A "where to find what" index shared with the team

Encourage your team to document *as they go*, not just when asked, and then update it quarterly—with pride! Not about micromanagement, it's about clarity so that when someone leaves, you don't need to hunt for passwords or guess what that presentation named "final_final_reallyfinal_v4 " actually means. In this way, you'll be ready to say:

> *"We're covered. Let's support [insert name here] in [his/her] exit while keeping the team steady."*

Documentation isn't just an insurance policy but in fact a sign of respect—for the work and the people tasked with executing it next.

They Manage Bandwidth with Honesty

When someone leaves, the work doesn't just disappear—nor can it be absorbed *like that* with a quick snap of the fingers. Too often, leaders redistribute work without any regard for...

- Capacity
- Prioritization
- Burnout risk

This leads to overwork, resentment, departures, and (eventually) even more exits. Great leaders do something *different*. They triage, reprioritize, and say:

> *"We no longer have the same capacity. That means something has to pause."*

Then, they create and share project tiers as follows:

- Mission-Critical
- Strategic but Flexible
- Pause
- Cut

They teach their teams to use prioritization matrices (e.g., the aforementioned Impact vs Urgency model) to filter noise from need, don't pretend everyone can "just do more," and protect them from the chaos that often follows a layoff—safeguarding culture in doing so.

Saying no to a project isn't failure. It's stewardship; the bandwidth you guard is the burnout you prevent.

They Lead with Clarity, Up and Downstream

Someone leaving your team? Cue the corresponding panic! Upstream stakeholders worry about delivery, downstream teams worry about morale, and peers worry they're next on the chopping block. Great leaders communicate proactively in *both directions*, saying to executives:

"With this headcount loss, here's what shifts. Here's what pauses. Here's the support we'll need."

And to the team:

"This is what happened. Here's what it means for us. Here's what stays the same and what changes. Here's what we're not sure about yet—but will tell you as soon as we know."

Then, they keep talking via 1:1s, standups, and walk-and-talks: all of which provide space for grief, clarity, and venting. Not just broadcasting, they *listen*.

When you lead with clarity, you earn trust. When trust is high, people stay—even when the winds shift.

Lead the Work, Lift the People

Let's dig deeper into the prioritization matrix concept I've mentioned a few times now. Beyond just planning, a matrix is designed to help develop your team's decision-making muscle and teach your people to ask...

- Is this truly urgent or just *loud*?
- What's the downstream impact if we delay this?

- Who's asking for this, and do they understand our current load?

Show them how to triage like leaders—not just task managers—to keep your team from being pulled into performative hustle. This gives them the language to push back professionally, saying things like....

> *"That's a Q3 priority. We've tiered it in the 'Plan & Schedule' category for now."*

> *"Given current capacity, we're pausing this as a low-impact/low-urgency matter until we wrap critical deliverables."*

> *"If we take this on, we'll need to pause [x]. Let's align before moving forward."*

Not just managing work, you're teaching resilience.

Your team should never have to choose between excellence and exhaustion. Give them a framework that guards *both*.

Because Leaving Is Part of Leading

Why do people continue to act as if exits are shocking? As if someone eventually moving on is a mind-boggling phenomenon and a deep form of betrayal? The truth is that people leave roles all the time, and the best teams aren't the ones who *never* experience turnover but the ones who do so without falling apart.

Your goal, likewise, is not to prevent every departure but instead build a team where...

- People feel proud of what they've built
- Documentation lives beyond any one person
- Priorities are clear, shared, and human
- No one scrambles to pretend everything's fine

The best leadership isn't reactive. It's *ready*.

Remember...

Empty seats will exist from time to time. Lead like that's not a threat but a truth you've prepared for.

5

Speaking Up as an Advocate, Ally, and Interrupter

You didn't make the decision. But you *can* choose to challenge the default.

Layoffs can feel so, well, *immovable*. There's the business case built, the finance model finalized, the C-suite decision made, and the script handed down. By the time you're looped in, you may feel like a messenger—not a leader. Yet this is in fact still your role!

Leaders don't just deliver decisions; they shape them, question them, and interrupt them when harm is rushed through for the sake of speed. Sometimes you need to speak up—not to be disruptive but to be *discerning*—as someone who believes layoffs need not be cruel, careless, or culturally corrosive even if they're necessary.

Even if you didn't choose the cut, you're still responsible for how it happens.

Powerless? Nope!

Let's make something plain: Most leaders in an organization don't get to decide if a layoff will happen. This decision typically comes from...

- The executive suite
- Finance leaders
- Board mandates
- External pressures (market shifts, M&A, investor demands, etc.)

Here's what leaders *can* influence:

- How people are selected
- How the message is delivered
- What support is offered
- What happens to the work and the team in the aftermath
- How the moment is memorialized and processed

That's more power than you may realize. How you use it ultimately defines your leadership.

The "I Wasn't in the Room" Excuse

It's the default phrase leaders use when a layoff rolls downhill:

"I just found out yesterday."

"I wasn't there."

"It wasn't my call."

While this may be true, what people hear is:

"I'm not responsible for how you feel about this."

This is what damages trust, *especially* among the people who look to you for leadership beyond cookie-cutter updates. Not in the room when the decision was made? Doesn't matter! Be the one who...

- Brings humanity back into the rollout
- Offers clarity, context, and care
- Protects your team from avoidable harm

You don't need to be the decision-maker to be a culture-shaper.

Interruption Is Not Insurrection

Turns out, you can indeed speak up without blowing things up. While a common myth says challenging decisions label you as a troublemaker, the very best cultures invite challenge in reality. Leaders who ask the right questions aren't a threat to the business but a *gift* to the people.

You, likewise, can use your voice to help avoid harm, clarify strategy, and keep values centered when a layoff is being planned or already in motion. Here's a list of related questions to bring to your peers, HR, or executive sponsors spanning various categories...

Strategy + Selection

- "What criteria are we using to select impacted roles? Performance, redundancy, or geography?"
- "How can we ensure this process is equitable, not just convenient?"
- "Have we considered how this will affect underrepresented groups, remote workers, or parents?"

Messaging + Communication

- "How are we preparing managers to have this conversation?"
- "Will we send out a statement that matches our company values?"

- "Will the message make sense to the person receiving it, or just to Legal?"

Support + Dignity

- "What are we offering beyond severance?"
- "Are we offering resume support, references, or time to transition?"
- "Have we considered time of day, time zone, and sensitivity of delivery?"

Culture + Aftermath

- "What's our plan for the team that remains?"
- "How will we explain this to the company without minimizing what happened?"
- "Are we creating space for grieving, rebuilding, or even just asking questions?"

Not rebellious questions, they're *responsible* questions that change the room.

Being Heard Without Being Dismissed

It's one thing to ask the hard questions, but you'll also need to do it in a way that gets you invited back to the table. To speak up effectively...

Stay grounded in values, not venting.

- Wrong: "This feels wrong."
- Right: "This feels misaligned with our value of transparency. How can we address that?"

Anchor in impact, not emotion alone.

- Wrong: "This is going to upset people."
- Right: "This may erode trust if we don't explain the *why* clearly. Can we revise the messaging?"

Position yourself as a partner, not a critic.

- Wrong: "This is going to backfire."
- Right: "I'd love to help us think through the employee experience, especially for the rollout."

Come with suggestions, not just pushback.

- Wrong: "This won't work."
- Right: "What if we built in a buffer week for knowledge transfer or offered structured offboarding support?"

When you speak up with composure, clarity, and commitment to the culture, you *build* credibility rather than risk it.

Leadership = Loudness? Not Always

Advocacy need not be some sort of dramatic boardroom moment, big speech, or last-minute save. Sometimes, it's just...

- The private message to a peer that says, "Hey! Are we sure this aligns with our DEI commitments?"
- The simple email that proposes a reworded message to reflect more empathy
- The 15-minute prep call with a frontline leader who's about to deliver the trickiest message of his/her career
- The moment you say to HR, "Let's make sure we don't do this alone."

These aren't headline-worthy moments, but they build trust, prevent harm, and reinforce culture nonetheless—and your team will remember you because of them.

Things Already In Motion?

What happens if you walk into the process too late, with the decision already made, the names selected, and the calendar invites sent? You can still lead, influencing how it all plays out (even if you can't undo the decision) with respect to...

- How the message is delivered
- How much context is given
- What's said in the follow-up
- What the team hears afterward
- What you say, share, and signal

Ask:

"Can I sit in on this call with you so the person isn't alone?"

"Can we add 15 minutes to the calendar so this doesn't feel rushed?"

"Can we draft a team message that acknowledges the person's contribution?"

Small moves? Sure, but ones that have *massive* meaning. Despite your inability to stop the cut, you *can* stop the coldness.

Knowing When to Push, Influence, and Stay Steady

Not every moment calls for disruption; some call for presence and simply being the most human person in the room, while others are locked into scripts. Others require persistence and a willingness to keep bringing up the uncomfortable thing no one wants to slow down for. Sometimes advocacy is the name of the (long) game, such as in these scenarios...

- Building relationships with Finance so they'll loop you in earlier next time
- Training your team on values-aligned decision-making *before* the next cut
- Shifting performance reviews to measure legacy, not just output
- Creating recognition rituals that make people feel seen even if they leave

Advocacy goes beyond the layoff moment itself as a way to lay the groundwork both before and after for a more just, human way of leading.

Here's the catch, though: if your advocacy becomes about you being right, you'll lose trust. You're not here to "win the argument," likewise, but instead to dial back the harm, protect your people, and build a culture you believe in. So check your tone, speak from conviction (not condescension), and lead with curiosity (not contempt). Ask yourself: *Is this for them or about how I want to be seen?* Good advocacy is grounded in service, strength, focused action, and values lived out loud—not ego.

The Ripple Effect

While you may not be able to change the whole company, you *can* change how...

- Your team delivers bad news
- Your peers speak about "resource cuts"
- HR is included—and supported
- Your people are treated in their most vulnerable moment

Such changes ripple outward, building a reputation, pattern, and story as you become the kind of leader people trust in crisis—not just because you're good in a room but because you don't abandon your values as soon as they're tested.

Leadership Is What You Allow and What You Challenge

You'll always feel pressured to "get through it," but what if you go beyond this to shape it and say...

"Let's slow down and look at this again."

"This doesn't sound like us. Can we rewrite it?"

"We owe people more than efficiency but dignity as well."

The world doesn't need more passive leaders. It needs ones who are *awake* and who will speak up, stay steady, and stick to their values even when it's inconvenient. That's precisely what it means to lead through layoffs with your *whole self*—not just your title.

Remember...

Leadership isn't just what you say yes to. It's what you're willing to question, especially when no one else is.

6

Say It Like You Mean/Lead It (Because You Do!)

What you say during a layoff is important, but *how* you say it is what people remember.

Layoffs are emotional—and they should be! After all, they're not just business announcements but in fact personal inflection points interrupting someone's plan, shaking his/her identity to the very core, and testing trust in leadership. Your words matter more than ever in these moments: not just the ones in your official statement or follow-up email but in the tone, timing, posture, and presence you bring to *all* of it.

When people are hurt, confused, or in shock, they don't remember the bullet points; they remember the *feeling* you left them with.

Not a Messaging Task But a Leadership Test

While there's no perfect way to say "Your job is ending," there *is* a way to do it in a way that keeps dignity intact, clarity front and center, and your own leadership aligned with your values. Yet this is the part so many leaders stumble through!

They copy-paste scripts, outsource empathy, freeze and ramble, over-explain or under-communicate, and say things they don't mean just to fill the silence. We've all seen it. Maybe you've *done* it. You're not alone, and guess what? You can do better, I promise!

To help you get there, let's talk about some common phrases that show up during layoffs and why they often *hurt more than they help.*

"It's not personal. It's just business."

Why it misses: Layoffs may be business decisions, but they *land personally*. This particular phrase can feel dismissive, even if it's meant to defuse tension.

What to say instead: "Please know this is a business decision and does not diminish your contributions."

"We'll all have to pick up the slack."

Why it misses: This statement piles emotional and

operational burden onto those who remain, breeding resentment and burnout.

What to say instead: "We're adjusting scope and priorities so no one is overwhelmed. If something needs to pause, we'll say so. Don't worry! You're not expected to do it all."

"We didn't want to do this, but we had no choice."

Why it misses: It removes leadership ownership and implies weakness or blame-shifting.

What to say instead: "This was a decision made with seriousness and care. It's difficult but aligned with what the business needs in this next chapter."

"If you have questions, talk to HR."

Why it misses: This sounds like avoidance and makes HR a shield instead of a partner.

What to say instead: "I'm available to talk, and our HR Business Partner is here to help, too, with logistics and next steps. You're not on your own in this."

"We're a family, and we'll get through this together."

Why it misses: The "family" metaphor rings false during layoffs. Families don't fire each other, after all.

What to say instead: "We're a team, and that means showing up for each other in every season—including the hard ones."

The Formula: Clear + Compassionate + Confident

Think of your layoff message like a three-legged stool. What happens if a leg is missing? That's right! The stool (message) collapses. With this in mind, make sure all "legs" are intact...

1. **Clarity**: What's happening. Why. What to expect next.

Avoid ambiguity, passive voice, or spin.

2. **Compassion**: Human tone. Acknowledgment of emotion. Respect for the person.

Avoid robotic delivery or too much corporate polish.

3. **Confidence**: Calm, grounded tone. Ownership of the moment.

Avoid hedging, panic, or over-defending the decision.

The Anatomy of a Good Message

Knowing you don't need a TED Talk but a steady story, check out this sample structure for a productive one-on-one layoff conversation...

1. **Open with Directness & Care:** "Thank you for making time today. I have some difficult news to share."
2. **Clearly Name the Decision:** "Your role is being eliminated as part of a restructuring. I know this may be a lot to process."
3. **Acknowledge the Impact:** "This is not a reflection of your value or work. You've contributed a great deal, and I want to acknowledge that."
4. **Clarify Next Steps:** "You'll receive an email shortly outlining your exit package. Our HR Business Partner is here to help walk through that with you."
5. **Give Space:** "You may have questions now and/or later. Either way, we're here to support you."
6. **Express Gratitude & Presence:** "I'm grateful for everything you've done here and can keep chatting if you want to talk through anything, or we can take a pause."

Don't Perform Empathy. *Practice* It.

People can tell when you're faking it—so don't! If you don't know what to say, you can keep it at that: "I know no words make this easier, but I'm here, and I care."

Empathy isn't crying on cue but showing up fully present, listening without interruption, allowing for silence, and holding space without rushing to a fix. It's also not making it about you, meaning you'll need to avoid discussing how hard the layoff is for *you* in the middle of someone else's heartbreak (which is emotional outsourcing, not empathy).

With all of this in mind, here's what not to say and some "HR-approved" translations...

You'll bounce back.

HR Translation: You may not feel okay today, and that's okay. We'll help where we can.

I know how you feel.

HR Translation: This news may land in different ways. I want to respect how it's showing up for *you*.

You're talented. You'll find something.

HR Translation: You've made a real impact here, and that matters. What's happening right now doesn't erase that.

Let's keep this quick.

HR Translation: This is hard news, and I'm here to walk through it with you.

At least you get severance.

HR Translation: If you have questions about the package, HR can help—but first, I want to make sure you're okay.

How You Tell the Team

As previously mentioned, post-layoff moments are critical not only for the person who left but for those who remain. Don't go silent during this time! As to not give your team any chance to whip up their own stories—usually unkind ones—include the following in your follow-up message or team meeting...

- **What happened (briefly, respectfully):** "As you know, there's been a change to our team structure..."

- **What it means for your team:** "Here's how we're adjusting scope and focus..."

- **What it doesn't mean:** "This wasn't performance-based and doesn't signal more changes to our team right now."

- **What to do if people are struggling:** "If you have questions or emotions, I want to make space for that."

- **How you're showing up:** "I'm here. We'll move forward, but not by pretending this didn't happen."

As it relates to values, if your company values say "People First," then *speak* like it—not hiding behind legalese if transparency is a core principle as well. Here's a quick alignment check for your message...

- Would I say this to someone I respect deeply?
- Would this make sense if I were the one hearing it?
- Does this reflect who I want to be as a leader?
- Does this reflect what our company says we stand for?

If not—rewrite it.

Focus on Presence, Not Reaction

You can't soften every blow nor guarantee how people will interpret your message, but you can be clear and present as someone they'll remember—not for your perfection but for how you cared during a difficult moment.

The goal isn't to be the hero but to simply be *human* and lead like your words matter. Because they do.

Remember...

Don't hide behind policy. Don't vanish behind an email. Speak like the leader they'll remember—with clarity, care, and calm.

7
Post-Shakeup Leadership, Emotions and All

Layoffs don't end when the message is delivered. That's just when the feelings begin.

Calendar invites? Gone. Exit checklist? Submitted. Slack/Teams profile? Sayonara. The work keeps moving, and yet, everything feels different.

If you're a people leader, you've felt it: the odd stillness after someone leaves (*especially* after a layoff), how your team walks into the next meeting a little more guarded, and the way questions slow down and small talk disappears.

You've just experienced a leadership shakeup—an earthquake, if you will—with plenty of aftershocks set to hit the office in the aftermath.

Defining Moments Happen Here

Layoffs reveal what kind of leader you are *when it's hard*.

- Do you show up or shrink?
- Do you make space for emotion or push productivity?
- Do you name what's real or try to smooth things over?

People aren't looking for perfection in this moment; they're looking for *presence* and have plenty of questions to boot...

- Is it okay to be upset?
- Are we safe?
- Do you see us?
- What happens next?

The only way they'll get the corresponding answers is if you tell them, not all at once nor perfectly but consistently, genuinely, and *humanly*.

The Emotional Fallout: What to Expect

Every layoff leads into an emotional ecosystem, even if it was expected and well-executed. While each person of course processes things differently (as individuals do), familiarize yourself with some of the most common reactions and what they often *sound* like from the POV of those left behind:

Grief

> *"I can't believe they're gone."*
> *"It feels weird without them."*

Guilt

> *"Why them and not me?"*
> *"I had more PTO... They had more tenure."*

Anxiety

> *"Am I next?"*
> *"What does this say about our team's future?"*

Anger

> *"They were treated unfairly."*
> *"Leadership doesn't care."*

Numbness

> *"It's whatever."*
> *"Just tell me what to do."*

You can't fix these feelings, but you can acknowledge them. That's what people need most.

Don't Rush Recovery

One of the most damaging post-layoff instincts is the urge to normalize too fast, saying things like...

"We just need to move forward."

"Let's focus on the positive."

"We're lucky we still have jobs."

These phrases may seem helpful, but they land as minimizing, dismissive, or tone-deaf. Here's what to do instead...

- **Acknowledge the moment:** "This is a big change. It's okay if it doesn't feel okay yet."
- **Make space for conversation:** "If you have any thoughts or questions, let's talk."
- **Be specific about the plan:** "Here's what's changing. Here's what's not. Here's what we'll figure out together."

Lead the Conversation - Don't Hide from It

If you're wondering whether or not to bring up the layoff again—the answer is a resounding *yes*. Silence creates speculation, and the people who stay deserve just as much clarity as the person who left. Some examples of good things to say include...

"You may be wondering what happens next. I want you to know I'm committed to transparency as we move through this."

"This wasn't a reflection of that person's worth or your value. It was a structural decision, and I'm here if you have questions."

"We're in a recalibration period. Things may feel uneven for a while, but you're not expected to manage it alone."

Your words, of course, won't fix everything, but they'll at least create a sense of shared ground, and the trust will build as you follow through.

Bring Your Humanity Without Oversharing

Your emotions are a part of this as well—and that's okay! You may feel...

- Responsibility
- Shame
- Exhaustion
- Helplessness
- Compassion fatigue
- All of the above or something else entirely

You're allowed to feel, too, but it's your role to not collapse into your team. Instead, you must model what emotionally regulated leadership looks like. This means...

- You can say: "That was a really tough conversation to have" or "I care a lot and am still processing it too."
- You *can't* say: "I didn't want to do it either and fought for them and still lost" or "I don't know what's going on and am just as confused as you."

Lead with vulnerability, not volatility.

The Power of a Venting Framework (and a Timer)

Sometimes, people just need a space to say whatever's on their mind—messy, unfiltered, and real. That's precisely why, in my HR Business Partner roles, I kept a 5-minute sand timer in my office. Here's how it worked:

"You get 5 minutes. Say whatever you need to. Vent, cry, cuss, overexplain, you name it. Just let it out. I won't interrupt."

Then I'd flip the timer again and say:

"Now let's do two rounds of problem-solving. What do you

need? What can we try? Let's figure out next steps together."

This type of approach works because it...

- Honors emotion *and* agency
- Gives people a container for their feelings
- Makes it okay to express without spiraling
- Reminds everyone that we're human first and *then* tactical

You too can put this concept into action in meetings, check-ins, or even Teams or Slack-style convos (in written form with timed replies). The method isn't the point; the *permission* is.

Rebuild with Rhythm: The 1:1 Framework

As your team heals, *weekly rhythm* matters more than ever. Enter the employee-driven 1:1 conversation, your best chance to stay connected in real time, notice emotional patterns, and coach not just with urgency but with care. The agenda looks like this...

1. **What am I doing?** Brief summary of focus areas or current workload
2. **What do I need help with?** Blocks, escalations, confusion, or stuck points

3. **What are my accomplishments?** Wins (big or small) and progress to celebrate
4. **What's my next move?** Growth goals, stretch projects, new ideas, or upcoming transitions
5. **What do you need from me?** Open feedback, requests, or direction-seeking
6. **What are the questions/directions?** Space for clarification, bigger-picture insight, or "what's coming"

Guidelines:

- Engage in this on a weekly basis for 20 to 30 minutes max.
- The employee drives the agenda.
- This is *not* a project status meeting nor an emergency huddle.
- This is a touchpoint for connection, coaching, and momentum.

When done right, this format...

- Keeps people engaged without burning them out.
- Makes feedback normal instead of reactive.
- Builds safety post-layoff when people are unsure of where they stand.
- Helps you see who might be struggling or otherwise shining.

All of this feeds into the fact that your team isn't looking for flawless leadership on the heels of a layoff but instead *true* leadership: the kind that shows up, names what's hard, makes space, and listens twice before responding once. With you as the thermostat—not the thermometer—you'll want to set the emotional temperature with calm, clarity and an open door. Amidst such incredibly tough decisions, how you carry your people tells them everything they need to know.

Remember...

The conversation doesn't end when someone leaves. This is when real leadership begins.

8

The Rebuild: Reengaging, Rebalancing, and Resetting

Layoffs Take Minutes. Rebuilding Trust Takes Intention

Congratulations! You made it through the layoff. Messages were delivered, follow-ups were sent, profiles were deactivated, and the dust has settled—or so it seems. Because here's what *actually* happens after a layoff...

- People keep showing up but not quite the same.
- Meetings feel flatter, wins feel quieter, eye contact feels harder.
- You're still the leader, but your team is not the same team as before.

Now, it's your job to help them reengage without forcing it, faking it, or ignoring what just happened.

Rebuilding Is the Real Recovery

Layoffs fracture psychological safety, even when they're handled well, quite frankly. Your people who are sticking around might not have walked out the door, but that doesn't mean they're fully present either. In the weeks following a layoff, you may notice...

- Slower response times
- Lower meeting participation
- Missed deadlines or unclear priorities
- Less collaboration
- More side chats and fewer questions
- An eerie sense of "let's just get through this"

Not laziness, it's simply emotional recalibration as people ask themselves...

- *Can I trust this place again?*
- *Is it safe to be visible?*
- *What's expected of me now?*
- *Should I feel grateful or otherwise update my résumé?*

If you pretend the recalibration isn't happening, you'll miss your chance to lead through it. Let's make sure that doesn't happen!

Quiet Quitting vs. Overwork: Two Sides of the Same Post-Layoff Coin

There's a trap most leaders fall into, only worrying about the people doing less than others or otherwise less than they used to do. After layoffs, though, two danger zones come into play—both symptoms of broken trust.

1. Quiet Quitting

Let me assure you: this now-ubiquitous workplace term isn't about laziness and instead about people simply putting their guard up. It can look like...

- Doing only what's required and nothing extra
- Detaching emotionally from work
- Opting out of stretch projects or high-visibility projects
- Avoiding conflict, challenges, or chances to be innovative

Your people aren't resisting you; they're protecting themselves.

Why it happens: They saw someone give everything and still get cut. They heard leadership say "people first" and then act otherwise. They're either trying not to be next or not to care if they are.

2. Overwork

This one feels like commitment, but it's often fear in disguise. It can look like...

- Taking on extra tasks without being asked
- Responding to every message immediately
- Working late to "prove" value
- Saying yes to everything, even when it hurts

Why it happens: They're terrified. They don't want to seem replaceable. They think over-delivering provides a safety net. They're trying to earn their seat *again*, even if no one asked them to.

Both are dangerous.

Quiet quitting, as it turns out, quietly kills innovation: overwork burning out your best people before you have any chance to replace the ones you lost. As a leader, it's your job to see both patterns early on and invite people back to healthy engagement.

What to Say to People Who've Gone Quiet

"I've noticed you've been quieter in meetings. Just checking in... Is anything feeling unclear or particularly heavy?"

"I know the last few weeks have been a lot. This is a safe space to talk about how you're feeling."

"You don't need to keep your head down to stay on the team. I value your ideas—always."

What to Say to People Who Are Doing Too Much

"You've taken on a lot lately, and I want you to know your role is secure. You don't need to prove anything."

"Do any new responsibilities you've picked up feel unsustainable?"

"I want to check in on bandwidth. Your health and comfort matter more than constantly doing more."

Parameters Over Pep Talks

I know it's wild to hear me, a cheerleader, say no to a pep talk. After a layoff, people don't need you to be a motivational speaker but simply to...

- Clarify expectations
- Provide a stable leadership rhythm
- Give them permission to pause or slow down
- Give them space to re-engage without pressure

This is the time to lower the noise and raise the clarity, which means...

- Fewer pivots and more consistency
- Fewer surprises and more transparency
- Fewer "Let's just figure it out" and more "Here's what matters most right now"

Reengagement can only take place when people feel safe, seen, and steady.

Rebalancing Work: Strategizing, Not Scrambling

One of the quickest ways to fracture morale post-layoff is to redistribute the workload without reevaluating priorities. If your plan is simply for "everyone to do a little bit more," you're not leading. You're gambling, which is precisely why you need to do this instead...

- **Run a workload audit:** Who's at full capacity? Who has room? What can be paused?
- **Map current priorities:** Re-rank everything by impact and urgency, sharing this map with the team.
- **Clarify what's going away:** Make it okay to stop something, permitting your team to focus without shame.
- **Create a "no" list:** List projects you're intentionally *not* doing right now, such as clarity, lowering anxiety.

- **Loop in the team:** Ask: "What feels most manageable right now?" "What feels like a stretch?" "What needs more support?"

Let your team help you shape what's next, knowing that a sense of ownership builds resilience.

Consistency Creates Culture

Don't expect a single, solitary all-hands meeting to heal the team. Post-layoff culture repair instead happens via...

- 1:1s
- Team check-ins
- Teams replies (or on whichever platform(s) you use)
- "How are you doing?" questions asked with the eyes, not just the words

People don't need a shiny new mural on the breakroom wall. They need *you* along with the "4 Cs"...

- Candor
- Clarity
- Compassion
- Consistency

Anticipate the Need

In post-layoff environments, people don't ask for what they need but instead wait to see if you notice, wondering...

- Will my leader still check in, or only when something's wrong?
- Am I still allowed to grow here, or am I just a placeholder?
- Will I be heard if I speak honestly about what's hard?

Want to lead the rebuild to the very best of your ability? Of course you do! Don't wait to be invited, and show up unprompted...

- Offering feedback in the absence of performance anxiety
- Celebrating wins without tying them to overwork
- Asking how people *feel*, not just what they *need*

Leadership in the rebuild phase is about trust deposits, little moments that say: "I'm paying attention. I care. I'm still here."

Belonging Before Velocity

The rush to restore productivity after layoffs is certainly understandable. You have fewer people, and the work, of course, still needs to get done. If you try to accelerate without restoring *belonging*, however, your team will spin out.

Rather than saying something like "Let's get back to it," try "Let's make sure you feel clear, supported, and prioritized before we build momentum."

With belonging as the launchpad for performance, teams that don't feel safe won't stretch, just as those that don't feel seen won't speak up. If your team doesn't feel centered, they'll drift. Rebuild culture first, and productivity will follow.

Closure Before Possibility

You don't move forward by pretending nothing happened; you move forward by naming what *did*. Even a short acknowledgment can help your team close one chapter and head into the next with a nice, robust sense of purpose.

"This team has been through a season, that's for sure. We've said goodbye to teammates, adjusted our goals, and had to deal with change. That's real, it matters, and I'm proud of how we've held it together."

Then—and only then—do you pivot to what's next:

"We're going to rebuild on purpose and do it slowly, intentionally, and with each other. You're a part of that, and I'm so glad you're still here."

You don't need a grand vision, but instead a grounded invitation to stay.

Rebuilding is Real Leadership Work

The looming layoff moment may steal the headlines, but the rebuild that follows is what will truly define your culture. It's where trust is either restored or lost, where people decide whether to lean back in or begin leaning out. Check your instincts, knowing not everything needs to be fixed or go back to "normal" right away, and that your team needs...

- Clear direction
- Breathing room
- Consistent leadership
- Human connection

They need *you*, not just to get them through it but to lead them forward.

Remember...

After the layoff, your words won't rebuild the culture, but your consistency will.

9

Make It All Mean Something

Layoffs shouldn't leave you bitter. They should leave you *better*.

As I've mentioned before, how you lead through and after a layoff will ultimately define your leadership legacy. You can let it harden and haunt you OR you can let it shape you. The layoff moment as a leadership inflection point— not an interruption but a teacher—is about transforming pain into clarity, experience into evolution, and lessons into new patterns of care.

Don't Just Move On - Learn!

With the layoff moment in the rearview mirror, you might feel tempted to close this book and simply get back to business. As much as you want to stop talking about it and start pretending like it was "just another tough day," you can't grow if you don't reflect. Layoffs *should* change you, not because you did something wrong but because you were trusted with something difficult and now know more in the aftermath.

What have you learned? What would you do again? What would you never repeat? If you don't ask yourself questions like these, you'll miss the leadership lesson you just earned the hard way.

Building a Leadership Debrief Muscle

Just like how HR and Legal hold a post-layoff risk and compliance analysis, you too need a personal leadership debrief. Try this reflection sequence:

- *What surprised me?*
- *What emotions showed up for both me and my team?*
- *What support made a difference?*
- *What went well?*
- *What felt awful, even if it was by-the-book?*
- *What felt misaligned with my leadership values?*
- *What would I do differently next time?*

Feeling brave? Invite someone to debrief *with* you! Whether that's a peer, a coach, or your HR Business Partner, you don't have to dissect every detail, but instead simply digest the overall experience. If you don't make any sort of meaning out of it, I can promise that it will still shape you—just unconsciously.

Share Learnings (Yes, Out Loud)

People trust leaders who evolve out there for everyone to see, so when the time is right, *share* what you've learned. There's no need to throw together a full-blown LinkedIn post or host a town hall! In your 1:1s, team meetings, and hallway conversations, simply let people see that the moment indeed changed you...

"This experience taught me how important it is to prep with people, not for them."

"I learned that silence after a layoff can create more harm than the layoff itself."

"Next time, I'll ask more questions upfront and speak up if something doesn't feel right."

"I'm now more mindful of how we divvy up work after big changes."

Not weakness, it's modeling that tells your team: "We don't have to be perfect, but we *do* have to be awake."

Transforming Insight into Practice

Reflection is good. *Reinvention* is better. Lean on this simple yet powerful activity either for yourself or your team...

Start/Stop/Continue: A Leadership Rebuilding Exercise

Name the habits, mindsets, and systems you want to evolve based on what you've experienced through the layoff process, using this after a difficult leadership moment or regularly during team recovery.

Instructions

Set a timer for 10 minutes, and reflect on your leadership actions, tone, habits, and systems.

1. **START:** What do you want to begin doing to improve how you lead through transitions? New conversations, systems, cadences, boundaries, or tools, perhaps?
2. **STOP:** What no longer serves your team or your integrity? Phrases, overpromising, reactive decisions, or culture bypassing, maybe?
3. **CONTINUE:** What worked well for you to hold onto and expand? Name and protect these bright spots.

Encourage your team to complete this too, then come together to compare insights: inviting co-ownership of the future beyond any sort of leadership dictation.

A Cultural Catalyst, Not a Cautionary Tale

Many companies treat layoffs like some sort of hush-hush thing, but what if you decide to treat them like a mirror instead? Ask yourself...

- *What did the moment reveal about our systems?*
- *What did it highlight about our communication norms?*
- *What culture gaps are now unignorable?*
- *Where were/are we surprisingly strong?*

From that clarity comes transformation. You might:

- Document better transition plans.
- Build stronger manager training.
- Rescope roles with resilience in mind.
- Shift performance reviews to prioritize legacy and documentation, not just output.
- Replace the "family" metaphor with something more real.

Whatever the change(s), make it intentional as part of a moment kickstarting a better way forward.

Your Legacy Isn't the Layoff—It's the Leadership That Followed

When people talk about and carry around how you showed up after a layoff, that's what'll stay in the culture and get quoted in 1:1s, passed down in team lore, written into Glassdoor reviews, and felt in the meetings six months later.

Make your legacy mean something.

Remember...

Don't just recover from the moment. Grow *because of* it.

10

Building Your Layoff Binder
(Before You Need It)

The worst time to plan for a layoff is during one.

Leadership isn't measured by how gracefully you manage your calendar, but by what you do when everything planned gets interrupted. Such moments—when someone resigns unexpectedly, you're told to make a cut, or a trusted team member is suddenly out on leave, for example—are when your systems speak louder than your statements.

While it's impossible to forecast every storm that lies ahead, you *can* prepare for them to the best of your ability.

Every Leader Needs a Binder

I'm not talking about a binder in the literal sense of the word—though it very well can be—but instead a mindset, shared practice, and structure that says "We care enough about people to not make hard things harder."

Some leaders think preparing for someone's departure means you're planning to push them out. Let's reframe that entirely! Such preparation is actually a form of respect...

- It respects that people have lives, goals, and timelines beyond their job.
- It respects that transitions can be smooth instead of chaotic.
- It respects the remaining team, who will no doubt feel the ripple effects of every unexpected exit.

Just as we build succession plans for our most senior roles, we should do the same for *every* role—not because we expect loss, but because we're committed to resilience.

What Goes in the Binder (and Why)

This isn't busywork, but instead "legacy insurance," the tools in this section are not just "nice to haves" but indeed essential for protecting your people, your productivity, and your sanity when hard moments hit. Let's build our binders together!

1. Role-Continuity Documents

Every role on your team is ripe for a blueprint that makes everything easy to pick up, not because people are replaceable but because no one should ever have to rebuild from memory.

What to include:

- Responsibilities (daily, weekly, monthly)
- Stakeholder relationships
- Access needs (systems, tools, administrators, passwords)
- Processes, templates, and recurring cycles
- "If I disappear tomorrow," need-to-haves: quirks, shortcuts, things only *they* know

When done well, these documents don't just protect the team but also help your *current* team member see the full scope of work—and identify opportunities to streamline.

Ask your team members to assemble these documents as part of their quarterly goals, framing it not as an exit doc but as a legacy handoff. What would they feel proud to leave behind when they depart at some point?

2. Folder Structure & Documentation Hygiene

The amount of work lost to "Where's the file?" or "Which version is real?" after a departure is staggering. You need a shared, intuitive, standardized documentation system to keep this from happening.

Checklist:

- One shared folder per team/project
- Agreed-upon naming conventions (e.g., "2025_TalentReview_Template_v3")
- Archive plan for outdated or legacy docs
- Owner assigned to keep it current (rotated quarterly)

Celebrate people who leave their digital trail clean, viewing a clear folder system as an act of leadership.

3. Bandwidth + Capacity Maps

Your org chart doesn't show real capacity, nor does your calendar. Instead, you need a living capacity map that shows...

- % bandwidth used by each team member
- Time needed for each recurring responsibility
- Mission-critical vs nice-to-have projects
- What gets paused when capacity drops

This helps when:

- Someone exits
- You need to say "no" upstream
- You're advocating for headcount
- You're coaching your team to work sustainably

Leaders don't earn medals for burning out their team. Protect bandwidth like it's your budget—because it is!

4. Prioritization Matrices

Your team shouldn't prioritize tasks based on who yells the loudest or is most senior. Use tools such as the Impact vs Urgency Matrix (available in the workbook) to...

- Coach your team to name what matters most
- Provide visibility to stakeholders
- Justify what you're pausing, delaying, or cutting

Then document these same decisions, knowing priorities should not live in people's heads (or stress levels!).

When layoffs happen, every "priority" will pop back up. Cuts not made visible will be quietly resurrected, so you'll need to protect your team from this cycle.

5. Exit Message Templates

Let's be honest: You don't want to find yourself writing a layoff message to your team from scratch at midnight.

Have two or three versions of these ready:

- Individual exit (due to layoff)
- Voluntary resignation
- Retirement or long-term leave

Each should be:

- Respectful
- Clear
- Aligned with values
- Reviewed with HR and Legal

It's not cold to prepare a message before you need it, but instead compassionate leadership. Panic planning, on the other hand, rarely reflects care.

6. Transition-Support Menus

Have a menu of options available for how exactly your org supports people who leave. This might include...

- LinkedIn recommendations
- Resume feedback
- Connection to alumni or talent networks
- Final-day celebration or recognition moment
- Offer to remain a reference

Let people choose the precise type of support that feels good to them.

You don't need a policy for kindness. If your culture can't sustain small acts of care, your strategy is missing something human.

7. Rebuild-Planning Checklists

Don't wait until after someone leaves to figure out:

- Who picks up which work

- How the team will be informed
- How emotional impact will be addressed
- How team goals or KPIs will shift

Make rebuild planning a repeatable process and include:

- A reassignment template
- Revised goal setting
- Team FAQs for "What changed?"

Letting go of someone without a plan for who's up next isn't leadership; it's erosion with a smile.

In Building the Binder, You Build Trust

Not about bureaucracy, the binder is about *belief*. A team that recognizes how you've planned for moments of disruption will...

- Feel safer
- Know someone is steering the ship
- Trust you to handle exits with grace rather than scramble

You don't have to talk about it each and every week, but when the moment comes, you'll be ready—which will matter in spades.

Plan for Humans, Not Headcount

Leadership extends beyond execution to stewardship, which means preparing for your team's full lifecycle, including the day someone leaves: perhaps by choice or otherwise, but when that time comes, you'll lead through it with steadiness, care, and a plan.

Because you built the binder, respected the role enough to honor the exit, and chose clarity over chaos and compassion over convenience.

It's what sets you apart.

Remember...

The work will shift.
The team will change.
Your leadership is what they'll remember.
Plan like it matters—because it does.

11

Building a Magnetic Culture

Your job isn't to keep people forever. It's to lead them in a way that makes them want to stay and be proud when they go.

Permanent retention was never the goal. The goal, my friends, is meaningful belonging while they're here.

That's it. End of story.

A good culture doesn't trap people. It grows them and gives them clarity, challenges, and the kind of experience they'll talk about for years—not because the perks were great but because the leadership was real.

We've spent most of this book talking about exits so far, but here's the truth: the way you lead before people go is just as important as how you support them when they do.

It's time to talk about the stayers: the quiet contributors, high potentials, and team members who are perhaps thinking about leaving but haven't said boo yet. You still have time to lead them well. Let's make the most of it!

Retention Is the Outcome. Relationship Is the Work.

Companies often treat retention like some sort of math problem:

- Reduce turnover.
- Increase tenure.
- Lower the cost of hiring.

Retention isn't about tenure, though, and instead about trust. People don't stay because of ping-pong tables or summer Fridays. They stay because...

- They feel safe to speak up.
- Their work feels seen.
- Their career still feels alive.
- Their values align with yours as their leader.
- They know you'll tell them the truth, even when it's hard.

The *best* way to retain great people is to build a relationship they want to keep showing up for. As for why people say and leave, let's simplify it...

People stay when:

- They have a sense of purpose.
- They feel emotionally and psychologically safe.
- They have room to grow or deepen their mastery.
- Their life outside of work is supported, not sacrificed.
- They feel led, not managed.

People leave when:

- Their growth stagnates.
- They no longer feel seen.
- Trust erodes quietly, one micro-avoidance at a time.
- Work becomes a place where they perform, not belong.
- There's no conversation about what's next—until it's too late.

Some people leave for reasons you can't control, but many do, in fact, do so because leadership got distracted. Don't be that leader.

Culture Built in Conversations, Not Campaigns

Culture isn't your branding. It's not your DEI statement, the mural in the hallway, or the perks in the app. Culture is whether...

- You respond well when someone says, "I'm struggling."
- People don't feel punished for setting boundaries
- Someone can say "I'm curious about a different role" without feeling disloyal
- Success gets shared, and failure gets coached

Culture is the sum of everyday leadership habits. Want to know what *your* culture is? Ask yourself:

- *How easy is it for someone on my team to ask for feedback?*
- *What happens when someone needs to say no?*
- *Can my team describe our values in behavior, not buzzwords?*

If you're not proud of the corresponding answers, don't beat yourself up! *Do*, however, build a plan to shift them.

Growth as a Norm, Not a Negotiation

One of the most heartbreaking leadership misses is when someone's already halfway out the door before you bring up growth. If you only ever discuss career progression when people are disengaging, you've already lost trust. Instead, make development a regular part of team life by...

- Asking about stretch areas in every 1:1
- Offering projects that stretch *skills*, not just capacity
- Giving people "preview" access to roles they may want someday
- Coaching laterally, not just up

Don't wait until they come to you with a resignation letter that says: "I just want to try something new." Give them that chance *before* they start looking.

Being afraid to ask "What's next for you?" isn't retaining but *hoarding*.

Talk About Leaving—Without Punishment

Most people assume they're not allowed to talk about leaving until they're already gone, which isn't culture at all. It's fear! The best leaders, however, create a space where team members can feel free to say, "I'm not sure if I want to stay." This, in turn, becomes the start of a conversation —not the end of a relationship. Try saying...

"If you ever decide to explore something new, I want you to be able to talk to me about it."

"I don't see leaving as betrayal or growth as abandonment and will support you either way."

"Let's talk through what you feel is missing. Even if this chapter ends, I want it to end well."

Normalize exits as evolution rather than acts of rebellion.

Coach Your Team to Think Like Owners, Not Tenants

How about a quick real estate metaphor thrown in for good measure? Tenants wait to be told; owners look for what's possible. To build a stay-worthy culture, treat your people like owners of their own experience. This means...

- Inviting them into prioritization conversations
- Letting them challenge the "why" behind decisions
- Giving them a role in shaping how their work shows up in the world
- Asking: "How do you want to impact this chapter?"

In allowing people to help design their own path, you'll help ensure they walk out the door *grateful,* not guarded—even if it eventually takes them away from you.

Don't Guilt Them to Stay—Invite Them to Belong

Fear isn't a retention strategy, plain and simple. Saying things like...

"You know it's rough out there."

"You're lucky to have a job."

"I don't think you'd find this kind of support anywhere else."

...might work on a short-term basis, but long-term? That's exactly how you create resentment. Here's what to say instead...

"You've added so much here. I'd love to keep building with you, but if your path changes, I'll still root for you."

"This team is better because you're here and will always be part of your story, no matter what's next."

That's loyalty, not out of obligation but instead *respect*. It's especially important given that when someone leaves your team, they're not just walking away from responsibilities but also taking...

- Your leadership imprint
- Stories they'll tell about how they were treated
- Skills they grew under your guidance
- Relationships they built in your care
- The legacy of how you made them *feel*

Whether they leave due to a layoff, a promotion, or their own next chapter, they won't forget if you celebrated them, made space for the transition, left the door open, and honored their time there as meaningful. People don't need to stay forever to become part of your leadership legacy; some of your biggest impact is carried by former team members as ambassadors, alumni, referrals, and/or future collaborators.

The bottom line? Don't miss the chance to transform exits into ongoing connections.

Keeping the Door Open—*Really* Open

"Let's stay in touch" is the business equivalent of "We should get coffee sometime." It only matters if you mean it. With this in mind, employ a real alumni connection strategy. Nothing fancy. Just *real*.

Examples:

- Adding people to a professional newsletter or internal update loop
- Offering alumni coffee dates or check-ins quarterly
- Celebrating their big wins on LinkedIn
- Referring them when you hear of roles that fit their new path
- Sending a "thinking of you" message 3 months after their departure

You're not their boss anymore, but you know what you are now? Part of their leadership story. Act like it matters—because it does!

Start the Conversation Now, Long Before Any Goodbyes

If your only leadership conversations are about the work in front of your team, you're missing the big picture.

Make career pathing part of your monthly 1:1s, asking things like...

"What's challenging and fulfilling in your role?"

"What part of your work would you like to grow or pass on?"

"If your dream role opened next quarter, would it be here or somewhere else?"

"What skills do you want to build next?"

Questions like these should be *normal*—not secret or scary —as part of a system that recognizes how people who know they can evolve *with* you don't need to look for growth *without* you.

Beyond managing a team, you're shaping a chapter in someone's career.

That might sound like pressure, and you know what? It should! Because if you're lucky, the people on your team will carry something you taught them *forever*. Will they say, "That's the place where I stopped growing?" or otherwise, "That's where I learned to lead myself in a better way?"

Your job, likewise, isn't to hold people back but to light the path, walk alongside them, and send them forth as stronger people than when they first arrived. That's what stay-worthy cultures do and what people-first leaders build: not clutching on to talent like a commodity but coaching them like it's your calling.

And that? That's a legacy worth keeping.

Remember...

Lead people like they'll stay forever. Support them, like they might leave tomorrow. Respect them either way.

CHEER: A Framework for Leadership When It Matters Most

Cheering isn't clapping from the sidelines. It's showing up when it's hard, and leading like people matter.

Layoffs are one of the most emotionally complex and publicly scrutinized things leaders ever have to face; most of them reach for whatever feels safe whenever they pop up. Things like...

- The script to make sure they don't say the wrong thing
- The spreadsheet to focus on the numbers instead of the people
- The speed to get through it as quickly as possible

Leadership isn't about reciting someone else's words or moving the work forward at any cost, though. It's about choosing how to show up when people are hurting and how to make meaning from something that, at face value, often feels senseless.

That's precisely why I've chosen to wrap up this book not with process checklists or sanitized talking points but instead a leadership model that's human: a framework you can carry with you not just through layoffs but through *any* moment when your people are desperate for someone more than just a manager.

It's called the **CHEER Model**—and no, it's not about pompoms or toxic positivity. It's about what's real, grounded, and what brave leadership looks like when the stakes are high.

Why Do We CHEER?

We CHEER because leadership in hard times doesn't need to be sterile but steady, clear, and kind without collapsing as we...

- **C**hoose clarity
- **H**old space
- **E**mpower exits
- **E**ngage the team
- **R**eaffirm legacy

Let's walk through each component, discussing what it looks like and why it matters.

C: Choose Clarity

When the message is messy, the damage is permanent.

People don't need corporate spin. They need the truth, delivered well but still *delivered*.

Clarity is:

- Saying "I want to be clear about what's happening and what it means"
- Avoiding phrases like "realignment" when you mean "layoff"
- Letting people ask hard questions even when you don't have all the answers
- Naming tradeoffs, impact, and next steps out loud

Why it matters: When people feel like something is being hidden from them, they fill in the gaps with fear. Clarity reduces anxiety, earns trust, and tells your team: "You don't have to guess where I stand."

H: Hold Space

You don't need to fix their emotions. You just need to stay present for them.

Holding space is the opposite of shutting down. It's letting someone cry without rushing, letting silence linger without filling it with small talk, and letting yourself be human—even when it's difficult.

Holding space is:

- Giving the person a moment to breathe before moving into logistics
- Staying grounded when they get angry or stunned
- Saying, "You don't have to respond right now. Take the time you need."
- Knowing that stillness is leadership too

Why it matters: When people feel dismissed during their most vulnerable moments, they'll remember it forever. But when they feel *seen*, even if the news is hard? They'll walk out whole.

E: Empower Exits

How someone leaves says just as much about your leadership as how they arrived.

Empowering an exit doesn't mean sugarcoating it. It means making the transition respectful, intentional, and resourced.

Exit empowerment is:

- Offering a clear offboarding plan
- Making time to recognize contributions (if welcomed)
- Letting people retain dignity, agency, and information
- Supporting next steps, not just severance

Why it matters: The person who leaves will tell your story. Make sure it's one of care, not coldness.

E: Engage the Team

Layoffs aren't just an exit—they're an earthquake. Your team needs to see you standing after the dust settles.

Engaging the team is about leading *after* the layoff, not disappearing once the meeting ends.

Team engagement is:

- Rebuilding priorities, not just redistributing tasks
- Talking honestly about the impact
- Creating space for grief, questions, and recalibration
- Re-recruiting people into the mission with honesty, not hype

Why it matters: People don't stay because everything is perfect. They stayed because leadership stayed *with them,* even when things were hard.

R: Reaffirm Legacy

When people talk about how they were led in this season, what will they say?

This is about looking ahead and anchoring your decisions in the values central to your own personal ethos and that of your company.

Reaffirming legacy means:

- Asking "What do I want to be remembered for here?"
- Tying hard decisions back to humanity
- Sharing lessons learned
- Making space for team storytelling and closure
- Leaving behind systems, not just sentiment

Why it matters: Layoffs do represent an ending of sorts, but they're also a beginning—of your leadership legacy, in this case, inviting people to decide what type of leader you truly are.

Using CHEER in Real Life

This model isn't a one-time tool but a daily lens. Use CHEER...

- **Before a Layoff is Finalized:** *Choose clarity* in deciding what to advocate for and why
- **During a Layoff Conversation:** *Hold space* and *empower exits* via calm, present leadership
- **After a Layoff:** *Engage the team* and *reaffirm legacy* thanks to communication and care

CHEER Isn't Soft. It's Strong.

Some might say this model is "too emotional" or "too idealistic" for real business. Let 'em!

The truth is that the leaders who change lives and protect cultures are the ones who CHEER: choosing clarity when others spin, holding space instead of hiding, empowering exits with grace, engaging what's left (not just what's gone), and reaffirming the type of leadership the world needs more of.

Be one of those leaders and the reason someone says: "Even when [your name] let me go, [he/she] did it right."

Conclusion

Lead Like It Matters—Because It Does!

Layoffs aren't just a business moment. They're a leadership mirror—one that reflects who you are when the script runs out and the stakes are human.

You've reached the end of this book—but not the end of your leadership.

If you've made it this far, you're clearly not the kind of leader who joined this work to deliver bad news. You came here to build something—something that mattered.

And somewhere along the way, you realized:

- People leave.
- Budgets shift.
- Trust gets tested.

- Scripts don't always feel human.
- Even with all your heart, you can't shield everyone from the storm.

You also realized this: you still have a choice.

You can lead through the hard things with clarity and care. You can face layoffs without losing your humanity. You can build a culture where people feel safe to grow—even if they're eventually asked to go.

That's what **CHEER** was meant to remind you of.

Because every choice to **Choose Clarity**, **Hold Space**, **Empower Exits**, **Engage the Team**, and **Reaffirm Legacy** is a choice to keep leadership human. Not perfect. Not polished. Human.

Keep Showing Up, Even When It's Hard

There will be days when the work feels heavy.

Days when you're asked to move too fast, cut too deep, or pretend everyone's "fine."

Keep showing up.

You don't have to be perfect—you just have to be present.

You're allowed to grieve when someone you care about gets cut.

You're allowed to feel angry when decisions feel misaligned.

You're allowed to pause a meeting to say, "This doesn't sit right."

Most importantly, you're allowed to change the game for the people around you—by how you model integrity, courage, and care.

Your Legacy Is Written in the Hard Moments

No one remembers how many metrics you hit in Q3.

They remember the people:

- You protected.
- You honored.
- You checked in on even after they left.
- You stood up for when the room got quiet.

Leadership isn't built in the easy seasons.

It's revealed in the moments when—

- You sit across from someone and say, "I'm sorry. This isn't what you deserve."
- You coach someone through their next chapter, even though they're leaving yours.
- You choose clarity over spin.
- You prioritize people over politics.
- You build systems that prevent future harm, even when no one's watching.

Those are the moments that matter.

Don't Wait for Perfect Conditions

You don't need an executive title to lead with care. You don't need a formal mandate to treat people with dignity. And you certainly don't need permission to keep the culture human.

No matter your role, you have influence.

Use it—to steady, to speak truth, to remind people they matter.

Make it your leadership signature:

People feel more human when I'm in the room.

They'll remember that.

They'll remember how you—

- Told the truth, even when it wasn't convenient.
- Didn't vanish when things got hard.
- Helped them believe in their future, even when it meant leaving your team.
- Made systems better, not just smoother.
- Led with both backbone and heart.

You won't get every decision right, but you can get the tone right—the timing, the truth-telling, the tenderness. That's what stays.

Leadership Is a Privilege. Treat It Like One.

Choose the path that lets you—

- Sleep at night.
- Walk back into the office with your head high.
- Know you didn't abandon your people in their hardest moments.

In doing so, you'll be the leader who stayed, steadied, spoke up, told the truth with tenderness, kept the culture human, and held the line—and the heart.

No capes. No viral quotes. No fancy titles required.

Just a plan, a spine, a full heart, and yes — that binder.

Go be the leader they'll remember.

With heart (and pom-poms),

Sara Bovey Covey

Your Corporate Cheerleader

Supplemental Materials

Appendix A: Managing Emotional Reactions After a Layoff

You don't need to fix their feelings. You just need to hold the space where they can have them.

This appendix is your quick guide to navigating some of the most common emotional responses after a layoff with grace, presence, and dignity.

Sadness

Tears aren't a sign of weakness; they're a natural release of stress, sadness, fear, or even *relief*. Your job is to stay steady, not stop any crying.

What to do:

- Pause. Let the moment breathe and give space for the reaction.

- Offer a tissue if you have one, but don't make it a performance. There are times when I purposely won't keep the tissues in the room, so I can exit to give them a moment of privacy to collect themselves.
- Say something simple like: "This is a lot. Take all the time you need. You don't have to rush through this."

What NOT to do:

- Don't apologize for the emotions ("I'm sorry you're upset"): *You* didn't cause the tears; *the moment* did.
- Don't say "Please don't cry" or try to wrap up the meeting more quickly because you're uncomfortable.

People will remember if you let them cry without shame. Be the leader who holds space, not one who shuts it down.

Anger

This is often grief in armor and can sound like blame, sarcasm, or outright rage. Sharp words or questions that have no easy answers sometimes accompany it.

What to do:

- Stay calm, not matching the other person's energy.

- Acknowledge the emotion without trying to defend every detail: "I understand this is deeply frustrating. You have every right to feel what you're feeling."
- If the conversation becomes unsafe, suggest a pause: "Would you like to take a short break or revisit this with HR present?"

What NOT to do:

- Don't debate, correct feelings with facts, or take it personally.
- Don't say "There's no need to be angry." There *is* a reason, after all.

Anger directed at the messenger isn't about you. Your calm is the real message.

Numbness or Flat Affect

Sometimes the person receiving the layoff message doesn't cry, argue, or react at all and instead goes silent: perhaps nodding and disengaging. This doesn't mean he/she is fine, but rather that the person has entered "emotional freeze" mode—the nervous system trying to protect against overwhelm.

What to do:

- Speak slowly and gently. Give space and don't try to *force* emotion.
- Offer something grounding: "I know this might feel surreal. You don't need to respond right now. Let me walk you through what happens next."
- Provide follow-up options: "Would you like someone from HR to follow up with you in a day or two?"

What NOT to do:

- Don't mistake quiet for compliance.
- Don't fill the silence by over-explaining or providing justifications.

Numbness is a survival response. Offer the space to process, and follow up with care later.

Disbelief

If someone says...

- "Is this a joke?"
- "Wait—me?"
- "But I just got a good review."
- "I'm on three projects right now. How can this be happening?"

...it's disbelief at work, a signal that someone's identity is tied closely to his/her work and the layoff is impacting more than just the role but indeed one's sense of self.

What to do:

- Gently re-ground the conversation in the present moment: "I know this feels sudden. I want to make sure you have space to process it. You're not alone."
- Offer next steps clearly and calmly: "Here's what happens next. We'll give you time and support to navigate what's ahead."

What NOT to do:

- Don't over-explain or try to rationalize the decision. This isn't a time for debate.
- Don't say "It's nothing personal." Even if true, it *feels* deeply personal to the person impacted.

When someone feels blindsided, meet him/her with calm, consistent facts and human warmth.

Appendix B: Top Layoff Complaints

Layoffs don't just break hearts—they break trust when they're handled carelessly.

This appendix outlines the top complaints people have about layoffs, along with actionable strategies to help you avoid them and lead with integrity.

"It came out of nowhere."

Shocked employees mention no warning, no performance issue, and no discussion—just a calendar invite, and then before they know it, they're gone.

What's really going on: People want to feel like more than a line item. Suddenness feels like betrayal, especially in the absence of company transparency about financial pressure, organizational shifts, or role risks.

What to do instead:

- Communicate the business context early, even if decisions haven't yet been made.
- Offer clarity on how decisions *will* be made (e.g., performance, redundancy, geography).
- Talk openly about how the company plans for uncertainty.

People can accept hard news. What breaks them is feeling blindsided.

"I found out in a two-minute meeting."

People mention conversations that felt robotic, cold, or rushed, having been read a script and then ushered out as a liability rather than a person.

What's really going on: People don't expect a party, but they *do* expect to be treated like humans—especially in such a painful moment.

What to do instead:

- Schedule adequate time for the conversation.
- Offer space for the person to ask questions or otherwise say nothing.
- Follow up later, personally or with HR, to check in.

You may have 10 of these meetings, but the person on the

other side of you may only have *one*. Make it feel like it mattered.

"No one acknowledged my work."

People complain about how years of service, countless hours, and zero recognition bled into an impersonal goodbye and badge deactivation.

What's really going on: Layoffs can feel like erasure when people aren't thanked, named, or seen for what they contributed.

What to do instead:

- Include specific appreciation in the conversation: "Your work on [X] mattered."
- Invite colleagues to share messages (privately, or with the person's permission).
- Offer a note, gift, or farewell gesture (if welcomed).

When you say goodbye well, you protect the morale of the people who stay.

"My team didn't know how to talk about it."

Existing employees mention how everything felt weird after a layoff: no announcement or any sort of closure, with people whispering, speculating, or ignoring the whole thing entirely.

What's really going on: People need help processing a teammate's departure, with silence creating confusion and disengagement.

What to do instead:

- Acknowledge the person's exit in a timely, respectful way.
- Share what you can about what's next—without violating privacy.
- Invite questions, set boundaries, and model openness.

Saying nothing *is* saying something. Don't let a vacuum fill with fear.

"I had to train my replacement."

Some laid-off employees were asked to hand off their projects to someone not being cut.

What's really going on: If the role is "eliminated" but the work continues untouched, people feel deceived and degraded.

What to do instead:

- Be honest: "The role isn't continuing in its current form, but aspects of the work *are* being redistributed."

- Be tactful and give the employee a choice regarding how to transition the work.
- Never frame a layoff as "your role is gone" if the job is simply being moved elsewhere.

Don't protect the business by damaging your integrity. Say less if you must, but say it truthfully.

"Leadership didn't show up."

People complain when the message came from a mid-level manager, execs never said a word, the departure wasn't acknowledged, and/or silence felt like abandonment.

What's really going on: When senior leaders vanish during layoffs, it tells employees: "We don't care—or otherwise just don't want to deal with you."

What to do instead:

- If you're not the one making the decision, still show up to own the experience.
- Be visible. Be steady. Be present in team meetings and follow-ups.
- Senior leadership should address layoffs broadly and directly—no euphemisms, no hiding.

Your team doesn't need you to be perfect. They need to know you're in it right alongside them.

"They said it wasn't personal, but it *felt* deeply personal."

People speak of leaders using "distancing language": "It's not about you." "This is a business decision." "Nothing you did was wrong." The corresponding impact, though, feels like rejection.

What's really going on: People's work is part of their identity, so telling them it's "just business" invalidates the real grief.

What to do instead:

- Say what's true *and* kind: "This role was impacted by structural changes, but your contributions here have been invaluable."
- Validate the emotional impact: "Even though it's not performance-based, I know that doesn't make it hurt any less."

The decision might not be personal, but the *experience* always is.

Appendix C: Leader Self-Audit Before, During, and After a Layoff

You can't control the business decision. But you *can* control how you show up.

This self-audit is designed to help you pause, assess, and lead better in the most difficult chapters of leadership. Whether you're preparing for a potential layoff, in the middle of one, or reflecting afterward, use this checklist to ground your actions in clarity, care, and courage.

Before a Layoff: Preparation + Advocacy

Structural Preparedness

- Do I have up-to-date role documentation for each team member?

- Is our folder structure, file access, and naming system clean and shareable?
- Has my team been cross-trained on essential functions?
- Have we mapped team bandwidth, project tiers, and task ownership?

Advocacy + Influence

- Have I asked questions about selection criteria and equity in the process?
- Did I speak up about any potential misalignments or red flags?
- Am I aware of support resources available for impacted employees?
- Have I partnered with HR, not just delegated to them?

Communication Planning

- Do I know the messaging plan, and does it reflect our values?
- Have I reviewed the talking points and practiced the tone?
- Have I been briefed on what I can/can't share and what I will share with care?

During a Layoff: Delivery + Presence

In the Room

- Did I create enough time and space so the person can process?
- Did I deliver the message with empathy and steadiness, not just speed?
- Did I avoid minimizing or over-explaining?
- Did I outline next steps clearly and gently?

Emotional Awareness

- Was I prepared for a range of emotions: tears, anger, numbness, disbelief?
- Did I allow space for a reaction without rushing or shutting it down?
- Did I stay calm, grounded, and centered?

Immediate Follow-Up

- Did I offer a follow-up connection (HR, peer, myself)?
- Did I note anything to debrief or address afterward?
- Did I take a moment to care for myself emotionally, too?

After a Layoff: Leadership + Recovery

For the Exiting Employee

- Was the exit acknowledged meaningfully (publicly or privately)?
- Did the person receive clear instructions and support options?
- Did I follow through on anything I committed to (reference, message, closure)?

For the Remaining Team

- Did I communicate with clarity and appropriate transparency?
- Did I answer questions without defensiveness or avoidance?
- Did I review team priorities and pause/reassign tasks as needed?
- Did I offer space for grief, confusion, and/or processing?

For Myself as a Leader

- Have I reflected on what I learned from the experience?
- Did I act in alignment with my values, even when it was hard?

- What would I start/stop/continue based on this experience?
- What support do I need to restore and reset?

Appendix D: What NOT to Say or Do

Well-intentioned harm is still harm. And in a layoff, the wrong words echo longer than silence.

No one trains you for the emotional precision a layoff conversation calls for. Most people delivering the message, likewise, aren't malicious but instead just unprepared, uncomfortable, or want to say something that makes the moment a bit easier.

Layoff conversations are not the time to improvise, though, and instead the time to lead with discipline, humility, and *restraint*.

What Not to Say

"This isn't personal."

Maybe you're trying to soften the blow, but it sounds like you're denying the other person's reality.

Say this: "I know this decision wasn't based on performance, but I *also* know that it doesn't make it hurt any less."

Don't try to emotionally distance yourself from the moment. Be present in it.

"You'll land on your feet."

There's no way to know that. The person in front of you doesn't need platitudes but *clarity*.

Say this: "You've contributed meaningfully here, and I truly believe in what you'll do next—but I know today is hard nonetheless."

Future-forward hope is fine, but don't bypass the grief.

"At least you have [severance, experience, good references, etc.]"

"At least" statements like these invalidate what's in fact a real loss.

Say this: "It's not the outcome we wanted, but I'm here to support you in what comes next."

"At least" often serves the speaker's discomfort rather than the listener's needs.

"This is hard for me, too."

Even if it's true, don't center yourself in the other person's moment.

Say this: "I can only imagine what this feels like on your end and am here to answer what I can."

Your discomfort isn't the headline. *Theirs* is.

"Let me know if you need anything."

It may sound polite, but vague offers put the emotional labor back on the impacted person.

Say this: "Here's who you can talk to in HR. They'll reach out proactively, but I'll follow up too."

Don't hand off the care. Follow through.

What Not to Do

Don't rush.

People remember when you made time—and when you didn't.

Be sure to:

- Block enough time.
- Pause after sharing the news.
- Let the person breathe before talking logistics.

Don't read the script like a robot.

Scripts are guidance, not absolution. Don't make it sound like some sort of legal Zoom.

Be sure to:

- Use the script to frame, not flatten, your message.
- Add your own personal tone, humanity, and acknowledgment where possible.

Don't over-explain or rationalize.

The more you explain, the more it can sound like excuses or spin.

Be sure to:

- Be clear, and then stop talking.
- Listen more than you speak.
- Answer any questions, or otherwise accept the silence.

Don't avoid the team afterward.

They see how you show up post-layoff. Silence breeds suspicion.

Be sure to:

- Follow up with a team-wide conversation.
- Acknowledge the absence.
- Re-center the culture.
- Keep showing up, especially when it's awkward.

Don't refer to layoffs as "rightsizing" or "rebalancing."

People know what layoffs are. Corporate euphemisms erode trust.

Be sure to:

- Use plain language.
    - "This was a layoff."
    - "Roles were eliminated."
    - "We had to make some difficult changes."

A Letter to the One Who was Let Go

"You are not your title.

You are not this moment.

You are not erased."

This is not how you imagined your story would go.

You showed up. You built something. You gave your time, your energy, your ideas. Maybe even your nights, your weekends, your best work. And now you're carrying a folder, a final paycheck, and a thousand questions no one answered in that meeting.

I don't know if anyone told you this yet, so let me say it clearly: **You matter.** You mattered *before* the layoff. You still matter *after* it.

This isn't a moral failing. It's not proof that you weren't good enough. It's a business decision that hit where it always does—personally. And now you're grieving. Even if you're relieved. Even if you saw it coming. Even if you're already lining up your next thing. Grief still comes.

Let it.

Let yourself be mad. Let yourself be numb. Let yourself replay every meeting where you went the extra mile and wonder why it wasn't enough. Let yourself cry when you log off for the last time or delete the badge from your wallet. Let yourself feel what you feel without rushing past it.

Then, when you're ready, I want you to remember this:

They didn't take your talent. They didn't take your growth. They didn't take your ability to make something meaningful out of hard things.

You still know how to lead. You still know how to build. You still know how to light up a room, a role, a mission.

And the people who saw you? Really saw you? They still see you now.

That includes me.

You are not the person who got laid off. You are the person who kept your head up when it happened. The one who tried. The one who showed up anyway. The one who, even now, is still looking for meaning and movement and momentum.

So no matter what happens next—remember:

This moment is not your undoing.

It's just your next chapter turning.

And I can't wait to see how you write it.

With heart (and pom-poms),

🖤

Sara Bovey Covey

Your Corporate Cheerleader

Workbook Companion

Introduction

Reflection is the bridge between knowing better and doing better.

How to Use This Workbook

This workbook is your bridge between reading and leading. It's not homework; it's heart work—designed to help you move from awareness to application, from reflection to readiness. The pages ahead are where you'll slow down, think deeply, and practice the kind of leadership that leaves people better than you found them, even when the moment is hard.

You don't have to complete it in order or in one sitting. In fact, I'd encourage the opposite—use it as a living companion. Come back to it before a big conversation, after a tough meeting, or when you simply need to remind yourself that leading with care is not weakness; it's wisdom.

How It's Structured

Each chapter from *The Way We Let Them Go* includes **three practical activities**—one for reflection, one for connection, and one for action.

- **Reflection** prompts are inward-facing moments to examine what you believe, feel, or fear.
- **Connection** exercises are meant to spark dialogue —with peers, teams, mentors, or yourself.
- **Action** activities turn insight into behavior. They're the doing part of leadership—the tools, templates, and tangible next steps.

You'll also find short **"Remember..."** prompts throughout. These are your leadership anchors—quick reminders of who you are and how you want to show up when things feel uncertain.

How to Get the Most Out of It

- **Be honest.** Leadership growth doesn't happen in polished sentences; it happens in the messy middle of reflection.
- **Be curious.** You might not have all the answers yet

—and that's the point. Curiosity is what keeps your leadership human.

- **Be consistent.** Come back to the pages that challenged you. Revisit the same exercise a month later and see what's changed.
- **Be collaborative.** Invite your peers, mentors, or teams into the process. Real transformation happens in conversation, not isolation.

When to Use It

- Before or after a difficult conversation
- When preparing for a team restructure or change
- During annual reflections or culture resets
- As part of leadership development or team off-sites
- Whenever you need to remember that leading people well is both a privilege and a responsibility

Final Thought

This workbook isn't about perfect answers; it's about brave practice.

Let the pages be a mirror, not a measure.

Let the questions be a guide, not a test.

And let this be your proof that care and clarity can coexist —and that your leadership can set a new standard for what "doing it well" looks like.

With heart (and purpose),

Sara Bovey Covey

Your Corporate Cheerleader

Chapter 1 Exercises

The Truth About Layoffs Nobody Tells You

This activity builds from the stories that opened the chapter—the three distinct moments where leadership either rose to meet the weight of the moment or collapsed under it. It draws especially from the section "When Leadership Fails the Moment," inviting you to slow down and notice what those moments reveal about care, clarity, and the absence of both.

This is your chance to reflect on the moments you've lived or witnessed—times when endings were handled with grace, or when they weren't. The goal isn't to judge them, but to see them clearly, so you can lead differently when it's your turn in the chair.

Reflection | The Moments That Stayed With You

Think back on a time when your role—or someone else's—was ending.

- What do you remember most about that moment?
- How did it feel in your body?
- What was said, and what was left unsaid?
- What did the silence communicate?

Write it down exactly as you remember it—not to relive it, but to understand what it taught you about leadership under pressure.

Remember: The details fade, but the feeling never does.

Connection | What Leadership Looked Like Then

Now step back from the moment.

- What choices shaped how that transition unfolded?
- Where did leadership show up, and where did it fall short?
- How did that experience shape what you expect— or offer—as a leader today?

Capture the patterns you see across different experiences. Those patterns are data about culture, care, and courage.

Remember: Leadership is revealed in how endings are handled.

Action | Redefining Care and Clarity

Use what you've written to redefine how you'll approach hard conversations moving forward.

Finish these prompts in your own words:

- *In moments of uncertainty, I will...*
- *When people look to me for answers, I will lead with...*
- *Even when outcomes can't change, I will make sure that...*

These statements become your personal guide for showing care and clarity in difficult moments.

Remember: You can't control the decision, but you can control the delivery.

Chapter 2 Exercises

How We Got Here (A Business Case for Broken Hearts)

This activity expands on the chapter's call to look closely at how "professionalism" can slowly harden into detachment. It asks you to notice where that same pattern may have shown up in your own work—moments when efficiency or optics took precedence over care. This is your space to slow down, name what you've seen, and question what "professional" has come to mean in your world. You're not here to fix the system. You're here to see it clearly—and choose differently next time.

Reflection | Where Detachment Shows Up

Think about a time when you—or your organization—confused detachment with professionalism.

- What did "staying neutral" look and feel like in that moment?
- How did it affect the people involved, including you?
- What emotions or instincts did you push aside to appear composed?

Write freely. You're not judging the past—you're noticing the pattern.

Remember: Being steady doesn't mean being silent.

Connection | The Language of Leadership

Revisit the phrases you've heard—or used—to make hard decisions sound easier.

- Which words or metaphors ("realign," "streamline," "right-size") show up most often in your world?
- What work do those words do for you? What work do they hide?
- How does your team talk about change when people are impacted?

Underline the words that feel empty or overly polished. Then list one or two that feel real.

Remember: Language is a mirror. It shows what a culture values when things get hard.

Action | Putting Care Back Into the Process

Choose one leadership moment—past or upcoming—where clarity matters and care has room to grow.

- How can you make space for questions instead of rushing to closure?
- What would it look like to replace "We'll figure it out" with something more grounded and human?
- What one behavior will signal to your team that you're present, not performing?

Write one commitment you'll carry forward:

"In hard decisions, I will..."

Remember: You can't control the outcome, but you can control how people feel in the moment you deliver it.

Chapter 3 Exercises

Great Leaders Know Everyone Leaves

This activity invites you to think differently about endings—not as losses to brace for, but as part of the natural rhythm of leadership. You'll reflect on how your team prepares for transitions, how you handle capacity when someone leaves, and how to protect both people and performance without losing care along the way. This isn't crisis planning. It's continuity building. You're designing a culture where people can grow, go, and still speak well of how they left—and how you led.

Reflection | The Roles Built to Be Left

Think about one role you've held or led that was never built to be left.

- What signs of dependency existed?
- What would have made the handoff easier for everyone involved?
- How might you redesign that role so the next person could step in smoothly?
- How would that redesign make the *current* person feel—more replaceable or more respected?

Write what comes up as you picture what it looks like when people can leave well.

Remember: Preparing for departure is an act of respect, not resignation.

Connection | What "Leaving Well" Looks Like Here

Gather your team or peers and explore this prompt together:

> *"When someone leaves, what do we want the experience to say about our culture?"*

Capture the phrases that emerge—the honest ones, not the polished ones.

Look for what people fear most about departures and what they hope would happen instead.

Those words reveal the trust level of your team right now.

Remember: People remember how they leave as much as how you lead them.

Action | Creating Continuity

Choose one proactive way to normalize exit readiness within your team.

It might be:

- Updating role guides quarterly
- Mapping relationships and key partners
- Building a shared process library
- Starting a "legacy log"

Write a simple plan or recurring reminder that keeps this practice alive.

Remember: Continuity is care in operational form.

Extra Activity | Capacity Math

When someone leaves—or when work simply grows faster than bandwidth—it's easy to reshuffle instead of reprioritize.

Let this be a reality check for your team's limits.

1. List each person on your team and their key responsibilities.
2. Estimate how many hours each responsibility truly takes per week.
3. Add it up. Compare the total to your actual capacity (40 hours per person, or whatever fits your model).
4. If the math doesn't work, it's not your people failing—it's your priorities asking for more than your capacity allows.

Use what you learn to guide real conversations about what can pause, pivot, or pass to someone else.

Remember: Math doesn't lie. Overload isn't loyalty; it's a leadership problem waiting to happen.

Extra Activity | Impact-Urgency Prioritization Matrix

When bandwidth is tight, everything can feel important. This tool helps you separate noise from necessity.

Step 1: List every project or task on your team's plate.

Step 2: Place each in one of four quadrants:

- **High Impact / High Urgency:** Do it now.
- **High Impact / Low Urgency:** Plan and schedule.
- **Low Impact / High Urgency:** Delegate.
- **Low Impact / Low Urgency:** Pause or eliminate.

Step 3: Review together. Ask:

- What's getting attention because it's loud, not impactful?
- What deserves time but keeps getting postponed?
- What can we stop doing altogether?

End by writing one phrase your team will use to check future priorities, such as:

"That feels urgent, but can we confirm the impact?"

Remember: Urgency gets attention; impact builds trust.

Chapter 4 Exercises

Leading (Well!) When It All Gets Real

This activity expands on the chapter's reminder that people leave for all kinds of reasons—growth, change, care, or circumstance—and your job as a leader is not to prevent departure but to prepare for it.
The reflections ahead help you examine how ready your systems, people, and culture are for inevitable transitions. This is your chance to step out of reactive mode and into readiness.

Reflection | Building with the End in Mind

Think about your current team or organization.

- Where are you still leading as if people are permanent?
- What processes or projects would be at risk if someone left tomorrow?
- How do you personally feel when someone gives notice—surprised, defensive, supportive, prepared?
- How does your team respond to change?

Now write one sentence that captures the difference between how you *wish* your team handled departures and how they actually do.

That gap is your next leadership frontier.

Remember: The goal is preparedness - not permanence.

Connection | Cross-Training as Confidence

Gather your team or peers and hold a brief "switch and learn" discussion:

Ask each person to name one aspect of their work they could teach others and one thing they'd like to learn from someone else.

As a group:

- Identify overlaps and opportunities for shadowing.
- Note where critical skills live in only one person's head.
- Decide on one area to begin cross-training within the next quarter.

Close by revisiting this question:

> "How can we make learning each other's work feel like development, not departure?"

Remember: Shared knowledge is shared security.

Action | The Single-Point Audit

Resilient teams are built on systems, not superheroes.

Use this audit to identify where dependency may be undermining stability.

1. List three single points of failure on your team—roles, tools, or processes that only one person fully understands.
2. For each, answer:
   - What's the consequence if this disappears tomorrow?
   - What's one step we can take this month to reduce that risk?
3. Commit to one improvement by the end of the quarter.

Example:
Risk Area: Client reporting dashboard
Impact if Lost: High – only one analyst knows it
Step to Reduce Dependency: Document workflow in the shared drive
Owner: Alex
Target Date: March 15

Remember: A strong culture isn't about keeping people forever—it's about ensuring the work can live beyond them.

Chapter 5 Exercises

Speaking Up as an Advocate, Ally, and Interrupter

This activity builds on the heart of the chapter: you may not choose the decision, but you can always choose how you show up inside it. These exercises invite you to reflect on the difference between compliance and conscience and to explore what it looks like to bring discernment, clarity, and humanity into moments you didn't create but still lead through. They're not about rewriting the past, but about preparing for the next moment when courage will be required—quietly, steadily, and in alignment with your values.

Reflection | The Space Between Decision and Delivery

Think back to a time when you were asked to carry out a decision you didn't make.

- What did that moment ask of you as a leader?
- How did you balance loyalty to the organization with responsibility to your people?
- What part of that process felt misaligned—or surprisingly right?
- If you could replay it, what would you do differently?

Now write one statement beginning with:

"Even when I don't make the decision, I still have the power to..."

That line becomes your anchor for future moments of uncertainty.

Remember: Influence often begins in the quiet questions, not the loud reactions.

Connection | Practicing Responsible Challenge

Use this framework with a peer, mentor, or small leadership circle to practice challenging up in ways that build credibility instead of friction.

Together, walk through these steps:

- Choose a hypothetical (or real) decision that feels off-course from your organization's values.
- Draft one venting version of your feedback and then one values-based version.
- Compare the tone, focus, and impact of each.
- Ask each other:
  - Which version would open doors?
  - Which one might close them?
  - What makes feedback feel like a partnership instead of a protest?

Finish by writing one commitment as a group:

"When we need to challenge a decision, we will do it by anchoring in _____."

Remember: Interruption isn't insubordination—it's integrity in motion.

Action | The Influence Audit

Even when decisions come from above, you still have levers of influence. Use this audit to identify where your voice carries weight and how you can use it more intentionally when hard decisions arise.

Start by reflecting on these key spheres of influence and jotting down your responses:

- **Your immediate team**
  - What can you directly control (tone, follow-up, emotional support)?
  - What can you shape (team morale, clarity, recovery after change)?
  - What action will you take next time a difficult decision comes down?
- **Peers and partners**
  - Where can you build shared norms or push back together?
  - How can you create transparency across departments or functions?
  - What's one proactive conversation you can start now to strengthen alignment before the next disruption?
- **Senior leadership**
  - How can you influence the framing of employee impact or values alignment?
  - What questions can you ask that invite reflection rather than resistance?

- What's one way you can show up as a steady, values-driven voice—even when you're not the final decision-maker?

Remember: power isn't only positional. It's relational. The more trust you build, the more influence you'll carry when it matters most.

Extra Activity | Questions that Change the Room (Group Exercise)

Create a personal or team "challenge bank" of questions you can draw from when a decision feels rushed or disconnected from your values.

Examples:

- What does this mean for the people not in this room?
- How might this message sound to someone hearing it for the first time?
- If we paused one day, what could we make better?

Add your own. Keep them nearby for the next tense meeting when everyone's moving too fast. Sometimes, the right question is the most powerful act of leadership you can make.

Remember: Courage isn't volume. It's consistency.

Chapter 6 Exercises

Say It Like You Mean/Lead It (Because You Do!)

This activity focuses on how your words land in hard moments. You'll look at the feeling your message leaves behind, practice translating common missteps into clear and human alternatives, and build a simple, repeatable framework you can rely on when the stakes are high. The goal isn't to perfect a script—it's to prepare your presence.

Reflection | The Words That Stay

Think back to a time when you had to deliver hard news or explain an uncomfortable change.

- How did your message land?
- What did you notice about your tone, your body language, or the space you left for silence?
- Were there words or phrases you wish you'd chosen differently?
- What feeling did you leave behind when the conversation ended?

Now write one phrase that captures how you want people to feel after hearing from you in difficult moments. Keep it visible as a touchstone for future conversations.

Remember: Clarity and compassion are not opposites—they're partners.

Connection | Practicing the Message

With a trusted peer or mentor, practice turning common missteps into moments of presence. Read each phrase aloud, then rework it together using clarity, compassion, and confidence.

"It's not personal. It's just business."

"We'll all have to pick up the slack."

"We didn't want to do this, but we had no choice."

"If you have questions, talk to HR."

"We're a family, and we'll get through this together."

As you rewrite, focus on tone and tempo. Notice how word choice changes not just the message, but the feeling in the room.

Ask yourselves:

- Which version sounds truer to your values?
- Which version would you want said to you?
- How can you practice this tone before the next hard moment?

Remember: You can't script sincerity—but you can prepare to speak from it.

Action | Leading the Team After the Message

Draft a short follow-up you could send or say to your team after a layoff or major change. Include:

- What happened (briefly and respectfully)
- What it means for the team
- What it doesn't mean
- What support is available, and how you'll show up

Test it with these alignment checks:

- Would I say this to someone I deeply respect?
- Does it sound like the leader I want to be?
- Does it match the values our company claims to hold?

If not, revise until it does.

Remember: Don't hide behind policy. Don't vanish behind an email. Speak like the leader they'll remember.

Chapter 7 Exercises

Post-Shakeup Leadership, Emotions and All

This activity helps you lead through the aftermath—when the announcement is over but the emotions aren't. In this space, the goal is to steady your team while acknowledging the undercurrent of grief, guilt, and uncertainty that follows. These exercises invite you to listen, notice, and rebuild rhythm without rushing recovery. The focus isn't fixing what happened; it's guiding what happens next.

Reflection | The Aftershock of Leadership

Think back to a time when your team or workplace went through a major change or loss.

- What did you notice about the energy and morale afterward?
- How did you personally respond?
- What did people need that wasn't provided?
- How did communication feel—open, closed, or guarded?
- What could you have done to acknowledge what people were feeling, even if you couldn't fix it?

Now write one sentence that starts with:

> "In moments of uncertainty, my team needs me to…"

Let this statement serve as your reminder of what presence looks like when the room feels uneasy.

Remember: You can't rush trust back into place—you can only rebuild it, one honest conversation at a time.

Connection | Naming What's Real

Gather your peers or team and start a conversation about what's changed since the last big shake-up—without trying to "fix" it. Ask:

- What emotions are showing up on the team right now?
- What's helping, and what's not?
- Where do people seem most uncertain?
- How can we make space for those feelings without letting them take over the work?

Record the themes that surface—grief, frustration, fatigue, hope—and look for the patterns. Those patterns point to what the team needs most from leadership next.

Remember: Acknowledgment is not indulgence. It's how you reopen communication after silence.

Action | Rebuilding Rhythm

Revisit your one-on-one conversations using the six-question format from the chapter. Before your next round of meetings, prepare by asking yourself:

- How can I show up more as a coach than a task manager?
- What signals might I have missed from someone struggling?
- What does safety look like in my conversations right now?

Encourage employees to drive the agenda and use your role to steady—not steer—them.

Remember: After a layoff, consistency is care. People heal through rhythm, not rush.

Extra Activity | The Five-Minute Framework

Try the venting timer approach introduced in this chapter. It's a structure for release and redirection that you can use one-on-one or with a team.

1. **Set the space.** Explain the goal: "You'll have five minutes to share whatever's on your mind—no interruptions."
2. **Flip the timer.** Let them talk. Don't jump in. Don't fix. Just listen.
3. **Flip it again.** Ask: "What do you need?"
4. **Flip it again.** Ask: "What can we try?"
5. **Close the loop.** Summarize what you heard and identify one next step.

Repeat this as needed in the weeks following a layoff—it's not just cathartic, it's clarifying.

Remember: Listening is not a delay tactic; it's a leadership skill.

Extra Activity | Leadership Temperature Check *(Group Exercise)*

Meet with a group of peer leaders or HR Business Partners and discuss:

- How are we setting the tone for recovery?
- What unspoken emotions are still lingering on our teams?
- How are we modeling calm without shutting emotion down?

Use the conversation to calibrate. Make adjustments to your tone, communication cadence, and check-in structure accordingly.

Remember: You are the thermostat, not the thermometer. The temperature you set becomes the one your team lives in.

Chapter 8 Exercises

The Rebuild — Reengaging, Rebalancing, and Resetting

This chapter is about the long game—how you show up after the shock fades and the silence sets in. The rebuild is where leadership gets real. These exercises invite you to reflect, reconnect, and reengage with your team in a way that restores trust through steady, intentional action. This is not about fixing everything overnight—it's about building something better than before.

Reflection | The Quiet After the Storm

Think back to the period right after a major change or layoff.

- What did your team need most from you in that first month?
- How did you balance getting work done with helping people feel safe again?
- Where did you see signs of "quiet quitting" or overwork?
- How did you respond to those behaviors—directly, indirectly, or not at all?
- What would you do differently now, knowing what you know about emotional recalibration?

Now, write one sentence beginning with:

"My team rebuilds trust with me when I..."

Let that become your leadership compass as you navigate the slow, deliberate process of recovery.

Remember: Trust isn't rebuilt through big promises. It's rebuilt through small consistencies that say, "You can count on me."

Connection | Reengagement Conversations

Pick two team members—one who's gone quiet and one who's been overworking—and imagine what an authentic, trust-restoring check-in might sound like.

Write out your opening lines for each:

- To the quiet one:
    - "I've noticed..."
    - "I just want to check in..."
    - "How are you feeling about things lately?"
- To the overworking one:
    - "You've been taking on a lot..."
    - "I want to make sure you're not carrying more than is sustainable..."
    - "You're secure here; you don't have to prove your value."

Afterward, reflect:

- How do you think each message would land?
- What tone and timing would make it feel most authentic?
- What kind of follow-up (if any) would build the most trust?

Remember: Your job isn't to motivate—it's to steady the ground people are standing on.

Action | The Workload & Culture Audit

Use this as a practical exercise to restore clarity and shared ownership post-layoff.

1. **Workload Audit**
   - List each person on your team and estimate their current capacity:
     - Under capacity
     - At capacity
     - Over capacity
   - Then ask:
     - "What can pause?"
     - "What needs support?"
     - "What needs to stop entirely?"
2. **Culture Check**
   - With your team, discuss:
     - "What feels most manageable right now?"
     - "What feels like too much?"
     - "What do we need to start saying no to?"
3. **Recommit Together**
   - End with a shared statement like:

"As a team, we're choosing clarity over chaos and steadiness over speed."

Remember: Workload balance isn't about fairness—it's about sustainability.

Extra Activity | Belonging Before Velocity

Before you reintroduce new projects or initiatives, take time to ground your team in belonging. Use these prompts to guide your next all-hands or team meeting:

- What's something you're proud of surviving or contributing to this past season?
- What does feeling safe at work mean to you right now?
- What's one thing that would help you feel more supported moving forward?

Collect responses (anonymously if needed) and look for themes. Then, craft a single message that reconnects everyone to purpose:

"We've been through change, and that's real. AND - we're still here. Together, we'll rebuild what's next."

Remember: Productivity follows belonging, not the other way around.

Extra Activity | The Consistency Commitment

To rebuild trust, make consistency your leadership brand.

Choose three small, repeatable actions you'll commit to over the next 30 days:

1

2

3

These could include:

- A weekly 15-minute check-in with no agenda
- A standing question in meetings ("What feels unclear right now?")
- A visible "no list" of paused projects posted for all to see

Remember: After the layoff, your words won't rebuild the culture—but your consistency will.

Chapter 9 Exercises

Make It All Mean Something

This chapter closes the loop. You've led through the hardest parts—the decisions, the delivery, and the aftermath. Now it's time to make meaning from it all. These exercises invite you to turn experience into evolution. They're not about reliving the moment but about learning from it, so the next time leadership gets hard (and it will), you're not reacting—you're ready.

Reflection | The Leadership Debrief

Every tough season offers lessons, but only if you take the time to name them. Use these prompts to guide your personal post-layoff reflection.

- What surprised you most—about the process, your people, or yourself?
- What emotions showed up (in you and in your team)?
- What support made a difference?
- What went well that you'd repeat?
- What felt misaligned with your values, even if it was "by the book"?
- What would you do differently next time?
- What did this experience clarify about the kind of leader you want to be?

When you're done, summarize your reflection in one sentence beginning with:

"Next time leadership gets hard, I will remember to..."

That sentence becomes your reminder that reflection is part of readiness.

Remember: The experience will shape you either way—reflection just makes it intentional.

Connection | Sharing What Changed You

Growth that stays private doesn't rebuild trust. Use this exercise to share your learnings out loud—in ways that model humility, not heroism.

Choose one audience (your team, your peers, or your mentor) and complete the following:

1. **Name one thing this experience taught you about leadership.**
   - "I learned that silence after a layoff can hurt as much as the news itself."
2. **Share one thing you'll do differently because of it.**
   - "Next time, I'll check in weekly until people start asking fewer 'what now' questions."
3. **Ask one open-ended question to invite dialogue.**
   - "What would help you feel more supported when big changes happen?"

You don't need a stage or statement—just sincerity and space for others to respond.

Remember: People don't expect you to be unshakable. They trust you when they see that you've been shaped.

Action | Start–Stop–Continue

This is your post-layoff growth plan—short, clear, and rooted in what you've learned.

START:

What will you begin doing to lead with more clarity, care, or courage?

(Examples: hosting leadership debriefs, building stronger documentation habits, asking "who's not in this room?")

STOP:

What no longer serves you or your team?

(Examples: rushing recovery, overpromising, avoiding hard feedback, equating productivity with safety)

CONTINUE:

What worked well that you'll protect and build upon?

(Examples: transparent updates, personal check-ins, modeling calm presence)

After you've written yours, invite your team to do the same. Compare notes. Find alignment. Then, co-create what the "next version" of your culture looks like—together.

Remember: Reinvention is reflection in motion.

Action | Turning Insight Into Impact

Take one final step by capturing what the layoff revealed about your broader culture.

Ask yourself and your leadership peers:

- What did this moment show us about our systems?
- Where did communication break down—or hold steady?
- What norms or metaphors need to evolve?
- How will we make sure this experience strengthens us instead of silencing us?

Then, choose one concrete change you'll advocate for:

"Because of what we experienced, I will..."

It might be updating your transition playbook, rethinking performance reviews, or reshaping leadership training. Whatever you choose, make it a promise that this moment meant something.

Remember: Your legacy isn't the layoff—it's the leadership that followed.

Chapter 10 Exercises

Building Your Layoff Binder (Before You Need It)

This chapter reframes preparation as an act of care, not cynicism. You learned that building your "layoff binder" isn't about expecting the worst—it's about respecting the people, processes, and partnerships that make your team work. Systems built in calm seasons safeguard dignity when disruption comes. The exercises ahead will help you examine how ready you truly are, uncover the gaps between good intentions and solid systems, and begin documenting the kind of leadership others can depend on when things get hard.

Reflection | The Systems That Speak for You

When disruption hits, your systems tell your story. Do they reflect panic—or preparation?

Take time to notice what your team's structure, habits, and documentation reveal about your leadership.

Reflect on:

- When was the last time your team faced an unplanned absence or transition?
- What went smoothly—and what broke under pressure?
- Which key details or processes live only in one person's memory?
- How do your current systems demonstrate care for continuity, not just productivity?

Now complete this sentence:

"If someone left tomorrow, my team would ..."

Be honest. This isn't about judgment—it's about clarity.

Remember: The systems you build in calm seasons determine how your people experience the storm.

Connection | The Binder Conversation

Gather your peers or team for a discussion using one prompt:

> *"If someone left our team tomorrow, what would break first?"*

As a group, explore:

1. What information would we scramble to find?
2. Which processes live only in one person's head?
3. What relationships or routines would be hardest to rebuild?
4. Which small steps would prevent chaos next time?

Close by having each person name **three binder elements** they'll commit to creating or updating (for example: role guides, folder hygiene, or a rebuild checklist).

Then share one realization aloud:

> *"I didn't realize how much we depend on _____ until now."*

Remember: Preparedness is not pessimism—it's leadership made visible.

Action | Build Your Binder Blueprint

Here's a starting framework to turn intention into action. You don't need perfection; you need progress.

Binder Blueprint Checklist

1. **Role Continuity Doc** – Outline responsibilities, workflows, and contacts.
2. **Folder & File Hygiene** – Standardize naming conventions and assign ownership.
3. **Capacity Map** – Track bandwidth, critical work, and what pauses when capacity drops.
4. **Prioritization Framework** – Use your Impact/Urgency Matrix to guide trade-offs.
5. **Exit Message Templates** – Draft respectful messages in partnership with HR.
6. **Transition Support Menu** – Document options for supporting departing employees.
7. **Rebuild Plan** – Clarify who communicates, who reassumes, and how you address morale.

Start with one area that feels most vulnerable and build from there.

Remember: A clear process doesn't replace compassion—it protects it.

Extra Activity | Legacy Binder Audit

Spend one hour conducting a *Legacy Binder Audit* for your team.

1. List each team member's name.
2. For each, rate (1–5):
   - Documentation clarity
   - Process transparency
   - Workload sustainability
   - Knowledge continuity
3. Identify your lowest-scoring areas—the "single points of failure."
4. Choose one to fix this month, and revisit quarterly.

This audit becomes your annual ritual of resilience, ensuring that when life interrupts work, your leadership keeps both moving forward.

Remember: Systems don't replace leaders—they extend their care.

Chapter 11 Exercises
Building a Magnetic Culture

This chapter reminds you that leadership isn't about holding people forever; it's about making their time with you matter. The same care you show during a layoff must exist long before one ever happens. Culture isn't built in policies or perks—it's built in how you lead the everyday moments that make people want to stay, and proud when they go.

The exercises that follow help you shift from managing tenure to cultivating trust—one honest conversation at a time.

Reflection | Your Stay-Worthiness Check

Before you think about retention metrics, think about relationships.

Use these questions to examine what it *feels* like to work for you right now.

Reflect on:

- When was the last time you talked with your team about their career goals—without a performance review attached?
- Do people on your team feel safe to tell you when they're struggling or curious about new roles?
- How do you respond when someone sets a boundary or says no?
- What does your leadership make people believe about growth—fear or possibility?
- When someone leaves, what story do they tell about you?

Write one sentence that captures your intent moving forward:

"I want people on my team to remember my leadership as _____."

Remember: You can't build belonging with metrics—you build it with moments.

Connection | Conversations That Make People Stay

Great cultures aren't designed in boardrooms; they're built through conversation.

Choose one team member (or peer) and use these prompts to start an honest, curiosity-driven dialogue.

Try asking:

"What part of your work feels most energizing right now?"

"What's one skill you'd love to build in the next six months?"

"If you could shape the next chapter of your role, what would it include?"

"What would make this team even better to belong to?"

Listen without an agenda. Resist the urge to promise fixes. Just hear them.

After the conversation, jot down two notes: one insight you didn't expect and one action you can take.

Remember: People don't stay because you convince them —they stay because you *see* them.

Action | The Belonging Blueprint

Build your stay-worthy leadership plan using the prompts below.

1. **Ritualize Growth** – Add one "career moment" question to every monthly 1:1.
2. **Make Leaving Discussable** – Normalize transparent conversations about curiosity and change.
3. **Map the Trust Loop** – List three small leadership behaviors that create safety (for example: feedback given early, boundaries respected, wins celebrated).
4. **Track Connection, Not Tenure** – At the end of each quarter, note one way you deepened the relationship with each team member.

Use this as a living document. Update it quarterly and treat it as seriously as you treat your performance goals.

Remember: Retention is the outcome; relationship is the work.

Extra Activity | Alumni Connection Plan

Since the chapter emphasizes that good leadership outlives the working relationship, create a simple system to stay genuinely connected.

Steps:

1. Keep a list of former team members you'd like to stay in touch with.
2. Set reminders for quarterly or semiannual check-ins.
3. Celebrate their wins publicly (LinkedIn, messages, shout-outs).
4. Offer support when opportunities arise—recommendations, introductions, or referrals.

This isn't networking; it's stewardship. When people feel celebrated after they leave, those still on your team see what kind of leader you really are.

Remember: Lead people like they'll stay forever. Support them like they might leave tomorrow. Respect them either way.

CHEER Exercises

The CHEER Model: Putting It All Into Practice

This final activity invites you to turn everything you've learned into something you can live. The CHEER Model is more than a framework—it's a mirror. It reflects how you show up when leadership stops being theoretical and starts being human. Use this space to translate ideas into identity, bringing clarity, courage, and care together in your own voice.

Reflection | Leading Through Hard Moments

Think back to a time you faced a leadership test—big or small—where people were looking to you for steadiness.

Use the CHEER lens to unpack how you showed up:

- **Choose Clarity:** What truth needed to be spoken out loud?
- **Hold Space:** How did you make room for emotion, even discomfort?
- **Empower Exits:** What did you do (or wish you had done) to protect someone's dignity?
- **Engage the Team:** How did you help others find focus and footing afterward?
- **Reaffirm Legacy:** What lasting story did that moment tell about your leadership?

Remember: Every hard moment reveals the kind of leader you are becoming.

Connection | Your CHEER Crew

Invite two or three trusted peers or mentors to join you in this practice. Each of you chooses one CHEER pillar you want to strengthen over the next quarter.

Together, discuss:

- What it looks like in real behavior, not buzzwords
- What derails it when stress hits
- How you'll hold each other accountable

Then write one shared commitment sentence that begins with:

"In the moments that test us, we will choose to..."

Remember: Accountability isn't correction—it's care with structure.

Action | Your CHEER Commitment Map

Translate the CHEER model into small, visible habits you can live out daily.

In the next week:

1. Pick one real meeting, message, or moment where you can **apply** one pillar of CHEER.
2. Name the specific behavior you'll practice (e.g., pause before replying, say what's true, ask one more human question).
3. Note what changes—tone, trust, energy, or connection.
4. Capture what you'll keep doing because it worked.

Repeat weekly for one month, then review your notes to see your CHEER leadership in motion.

Remember: Legacy is built in repetitions, not resolutions.

Final Exercises

Lead Like It Matters — Because It Does!

This isn't about wrapping things up neatly.
It's about grounding yourself in what this all means.
You've spent these pages learning how to lead through the hardest moments — with clarity, care, and courage. Now it's time to look inward and commit to who you'll be after the meeting ends, after the spreadsheet closes, after the storm quiets.
You can't always control the circumstances.
But you can always control your response.
These final reflections are designed to help you reconnect with your values, capture your leadership legacy, and remind yourself that people will remember how you made them feel.

Reflection | What You Want to Be remembered For

Think about someone you once worked for whom you still respect deeply.

- What made their leadership matter to you?
- Now, think about your own leadership.
- What moments—big or small—show people what you stand for?

Write three sentences that capture the essence of your leadership when it's at its best.

Then ask yourself:

Would my team agree?

Remember: Legacy isn't a title or a timeline—it's the story people tell when you're not in the room.

Connection | Legacy Conversations

Invite your team or a trusted peer group into a conversation about meaning at work.

Ask each person:

1. What do you want your work here to stand for?
2. How do you want people to describe your contribution when you move on?
3. What one behavior or ritual reinforces that legacy now?

Capture their answers and look for common threads.

Together, decide how to weave those values into daily habits—how meetings start, how wins are celebrated, how accountability feels.

Remember: Culture is sustained not by posters or slogans, but by the stories people keep repeating.

Action | Write Your Leadership Legacy Statement

Finish this sentence in your own words:

"When someone thinks about how I led them through a hard moment, I hope they say..."

Write it out, post it where you'll see it, and let it guide your next hard decision. Then, share it with someone you trust and ask them to hold you to it.

Return to it each year, updating it as you grow.

Remember: Leading like it matters starts with remembering that it always does.

Before You Go

You've made it to the end — but endings aren't really endings, are they?

They're proof that you stayed. That you showed up for the hard parts. That you cared enough to learn how to do them better next time.

You've reflected, rewritten, and practiced showing up with more clarity, more care, and more courage.

That's not small work — it's legacy work.

As you move forward, remember this: leadership isn't measured by how smoothly things go, but by how intentionally you lead when they don't.

Every layoff you handle with grace, every conversation you enter with honesty, every person you part with dignity —

each becomes part of the story you're writing about what leadership can be.

And if you ever start to doubt yourself, come back to this:

You can be clear and kind.

You can be strong and soft.

You can make hard decisions and still be human.

Because leadership was never about perfection — it's about presence, integrity, and heart.

And you have all three.

With heart and pom poms,

♥

Sara Bovey Covey

Your Corporate Cheerleader

www.ingramcontent.com/pod-product-compliance
Lightning Source LLC
Chambersburg PA
CBHW062200080426
42734CB00010B/1762